VIDENCE!
Citation & Analysis
for the
Family Historian

VIDENCE!

Citation & Analysis
for the
Family Historian

by
ELIZABETH SHOWN MILLS
CG, CGL, FASG, FNGS

GENEALOGICAL PUBLISHING COMPANY
Baltimore, Maryland
1997

Published by Genealogical Publishing Co., Inc.
1001 N. Calvert St., Baltimore, Maryland 21202
Second printing, 1997
Third printing, 1998
Fourth printing, 1998
Fifth printing, 1999
Sixth printing, 2000
Library of Congress Catalogue Card Number 97-72909
International Standard Book Number 0-8063-1543-1
Made in the United States of America

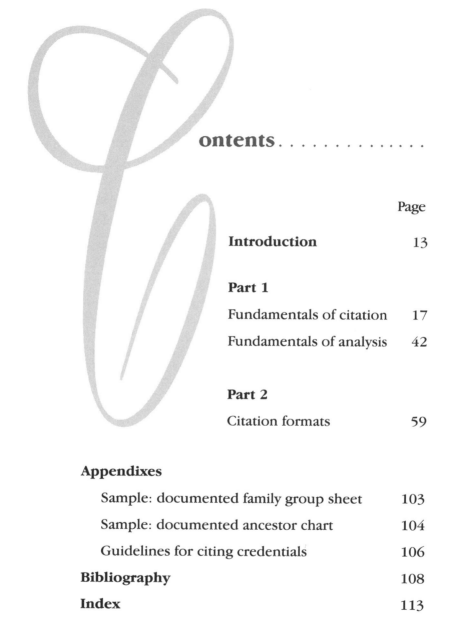

ontents . . . .

igures . . . .

cknowledgments . . .

Works that offer sound guidelines for their fields are rarely the product of just one person. *Evidence!* owes its existence to countless debates with numerous colleagues of wondrously diverse opinions. Many have helped to shape its content; others have road tested its citation models amid their own research and writing. The end product is mine, but it attempts to find a middle ground that mirrors the concerns, needs, and views of the majority and to provide a stable foundation upon which genealogical research can safely build.

For whatever role they played, I owe sincere thanks to Robert Charles Anderson, CG, FASG; Gale Williams Bamman, CG, CGL; Lloyd D. Bockstruck; Bettie Cummings Cook, CG; Joan Ferris Curran, CG; Donn Devine, J.D., CG, CGI; Mary Smith Fay, CG; David L. Greene, CG, FASG; Eric Grundset, MLS; James L. Hansen, FASG; Patricia Law Hatcher, CG; Henry B. Hoff, CG, FASG; Birdie Monk Holsclaw; Kay Germain Ingalls, CGRS; Helen F. M. Leary, CG, CGL, FASG; Rachal Mills Lennon, CGRS; Harry Macy, FASG; Rudena Kramer Mallory, CGRS; Marie Varrelman Melchiori, CGRS, CGL; Lynn McMillion, CAILS; Gary B. Mills, CG; Howard Nurse; Joy Reisinger, CGRS; David Rencher, AG; Marsha Hoffman Rising, CG, CGL, FASG; Christine Rose, CG, CGL, FASG; Elisabeth Whitman Schmidt, CALS; Craig R. Scott, CGRS; Kip Sperry, AG, CG, FASG; Jackie W. Stewart; Neil D. Thompson, CG, FASG; Wendy Whipp; and John V. Wylie.

ntroduction . . . .

Since its publication in 1981, Richard Lackey's *Cite Your Sources* has been praised, panned, and misunderstood. But it has been *used*.

Surely, no one's work has had such influence upon the everyday practice of genealogy. No other teacher or writer has made so many self-trained researchers aware of the importance of documenting the sources of their information. Yet in too many cases, his catchy refrain—*cite your sources*—has come to mean, simply, *cite something!*

Successful research—research that yields correct information with a minimum of wasted time and funds—depends upon *a sound analysis of evidence.* Source citation is fundamental, but it is not enough. The validity of any piece of evidence cannot be analyzed if its source is unknown. Citing a worthless source is an effort that produces worthless results.

Research, evidence, citation, and analysis are inseparable. Evidence is the vehicle that moves our research from curiosity to reality. Citation and analysis are the twin highways that get us there, smoothly and safely.

Evidence! tries to strip away much of the confusion that researchers experience in this adventure. It offers a road map for beginners, who hope to avoid mistakes, and guideposts for the advanced, who already appreciate the need to map their own course precisely. For you, I hope it opens new pathways to the past, removes the potholes and roadblocks for which genealogical research is noted, and rewards you with a realistic and meaningful discovery of the forebears who shaped both you and our world.

Evidence! stems from the belief that most researchers want to do good work. We simply need guidelines and explicit models—ones tailored to genealogy and to the original sources we commonly use but cannot find discussed in *The Chicago Manual of Style,* the *MLA Handbook,* or similar manuals aimed at a broader market.

As you consult *Evidence!* in the course of your daily work, please bear in mind two things:

- Effective source citation is an *art,* not a *science.* No formula can cover all situations that researchers encounter. If you understand the *reasoning* that underlies the suggested formats, you can devise sound citations of your own as circumstances require.

- Major publishers have their own house styles developed over years of experience in using the sources most common to their specialties. When we submit material to any publication, we follow its preferred style. The models provided in this guide strive to include all the elements that genealogy's major journals require. By recording this data in your research notes, you will have the essentials from which individual editors can fill their needs without repeated research on your part or theirs.

Above all, please remember that the purpose of source citations is not to create paranoia or anxiety but to eliminate it—by preventing mistakes and misunderstandings. We can all empathize with, but do not have to emulate, the student who once asked: "When I put my name on the title page, do I have to cite my birth certificate?"

E.S.M.

art 1: Fundamentals

undamentals
of citation . . . .

Ancestors. *Where did they come from? Who produced them?*

These are the most basic questions that genealogists ask. These are also the questions we must ask of our information. *Where did it come from? Who produced it?*

In the answers to those two simple queries lies most of our justification for accepting or rejecting the information we uncover.

The fact that words are spoken, or written on a sheet of paper, does not make them *true*. The appearance of a name, date, place, or statement of relationship on a frame of film— or in a database somewhere in cyberspace—does not make that information *true*. The past we explore and the people we seek are a fascinating spiral of false leads, confused identities, and tangled lives. As family historians, we inherit the job of unearthing every clue and weighing every fragment of evidence so carefully that we piece together an *accurate* mosaic of each ancestral life.

17

FIGURE 1

Guidelines for documentation . . . .

1. Any statement of fact that is not common knowledge must carry its own individual statement of source.
2. Source notes have two purposes: to record the specific location of each piece of data and to record details that affect the use or evaluation of that data.
3. Sources are tracked in two basic ways: by generic lists (bibliographies) and by source notes keyed to specific facts.
4. Source notes have two basic formats: full citations and short citations.
5. Source notes for narrative accounts can be presented in four ways: footnotes, endnotes, parenthetical citations, and hypertext.
6. Source notes keyed to narrative text should be numbered consecutively; the corresponding numbers should appear in correct sequence within the text.
7. Explicit source notes should also appear on ancestor charts and family group sheets.
8. Full citations should be affixed to the front side of every photocopied document and should appear on every page of a research report.
9. We should not cite sources we have not used; it is both risky and unethical to "borrow notes" from other writers.
10. Even a full citation of source may not be sufficient, legally or ethically, when copying from another work.
11. Microforms and electronic materials need extra treatment.
12. Clear citations require attention to many details.
13. Citing a source is not an end to itself; our real goal is to have the *best possible* source to cite.

This chapter lays out thirteen guidelines around which sound documentation is usually mapped.

ANY STATEMENT OF FACT
THAT IS NOT COMMON KNOWLEDGE
MUST CARRY ITS OWN INDIVIDUAL
STATEMENT OF SOURCE

Distinguishing "common knowledge" from a fact that needs documentation is really a matter of common sense. If we record that the Civil War erupted in 1861, that statement needs no supporting evidence to attest its validity or to help locate the information. Most historical researchers know the date, and anyone else can find it easily. However, a statement that John Smith enlisted on 23 August 1861 in Captain Hiram Jones's company of the Middletown Mounted Volunteers definitely requires a reliable citation of source.

SOURCE NOTES HAVE TWO PURPOSES:
- TO RECORD THE SPECIFIC LOCATION OF EACH PIECE OF DATA
- TO RECORD DETAILS THAT AFFECT THE USE OR EVALUATION OF THAT DATA

Most researchers recognize the importance of the first purpose, although the formalities of citing those specifics may be confusing. Part 2 of this manual addresses that problem.

The second purpose treats a quagmire in which good intentions are often sunk. As careful researchers, we need to enlarge upon many source citations—to add observations not covered by the formal citation and to discuss related problems.

The extent to which those explanations affect our judgment of a piece of evidence is a point made by the comparative notes in figure 2.

In short, genealogy is not a mere gathering of names but a search for truth—about ourselves and the forebears who produced us.

As we explore the past in search of that elusive truth, we must chart our way through the evidence we accumulate. At each step, *we must identify our source*—on each document we photocopy, each note we take, and each statement we make in our letters and reports to relatives and colleagues. Without this blueprint, only one result is certain: first we confuse ourselves, then we mislead others.

SOURCES ARE TRACKED
IN TWO BASIC WAYS:

• GENERIC LISTS (BIBLIOGRAPHIES)
• SOURCE NOTES KEYED TO SPECIFIC FACTS

A bibliography is an abbreviated reference tool—a nonspecific "master list" for quick consultation. It does not document any particular fact. Its primary purpose during research is to keep track of the materials that have been examined. Its function in a published work is to provide the reader with a convenient summary of the relevant resources.

Individual source notes—with complete and specific reference data— should be used when transcribing documents, making abstracts, photocopying materials, preparing research reports (for our own files or for others), and writing family accounts.

Part 2 of this manual presents models for citing a variety of materials in bibliographic and source-note formats.

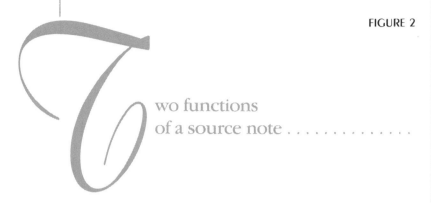

FIGURE 2

wo functions
of a source note . . . .

BASIC SOURCE CITATION:

1. Mary Doe, "Vital Records: Freetown Deaths," *Ipswich Genealogist* 1 (Summer 1974): 12.

RELATED DISCUSSION:

1. Mary Doe, "Vital Records: Freetown Deaths," *Ipswich Genealogist* 1 (Summer 1974): 12.

Doe's abstracts were not made from the actual vital records of Ipswich. Rather, they were taken from "Genealogical Notes of the Late Susie Smith," Smith Collection (MS, undated; at Anytown Public Library, Anytown, U.S.A.).

The folder containing Smith's notes is labeled "Ipswich Vital Records," but many of the given dates do not appear in the original vital-records register held by the Ipswich town clerk. The burial date that Mary Doe gives for John Doe is among the information *not* found in the original record book.

WHICH SOURCE NOTE WOULD HELP YOU THE MOST?

SOURCE NOTES HAVE
TWO BASIC FORMATS:
- FULL CITATIONS
- SHORT CITATIONS

In a narrative, the first time a source is cited, full details are given. Later citations of the same source use a short form that can be easily recognized and associated with the full citation (and with the bibliographic entry to which readers can refer if they do not recall the first use of that material). Part 2 of this manual presents corresponding models for full and short citations.

When we transcribe, abstract, or photocopy records, the use of shortened citations can be risky. If we take multiple excerpts from a single book, collection, or file, we should affix *a full citation to each sheet* of our research notes and each photocopy. With this precaution, if pages later become separated or shuffled, we will not be left wondering about the exact source of the data on any page.

Short citations should not be confused with three common shortcuts that promote writer error and reader frustration. If source citations are to be beneficial, they must be simple—easy to grasp, easy to remember, and easy to find. Consequently, good writers avoid the following:

- *Citing a source so briefly that it cannot be correctly identified.* For example, a "short citation" frequently seen in Louisiana-based genealogies and research notes is Mills, *Natchitoches,* 29 (or another page number). However, five volumes with "Natchitoches" in the title have been published by three different Millses. A slight expansion to *Natchitoches Colonials* or *Natchitoches Marriages, 1818–1850,* would take little more space and eliminate an identification problem.

    This pitfall is particularly acute in genealogy, where many volumes of local records are published by a single individual. As a rule of thumb, a short citation for a local-records volume should not only cite the author but also extract from the title any words relating to *place, type of record,* and *time period.*

One form of shortened citation common to scientific fields is unworkable in genealogy for a related reason: citing the author's surname, followed by year of publication and page number—for example: Humphrey (1989), 2—with the expectation that users will look up the full citation in the bibliography. Because many genealogists who publish record abstracts issue more than one volume per year (even several), the field of genealogy requires more-precise citations.

- *Reducing many source citations to acronyms.* This practice saves space, but it promotes confusion. Few readers can—or care to—retain a mental directory of KVR, QVRPX, LCTV, BWPC, LSNI, PMXE, and a dozen other mixtures of alphabet soup, as they study a writer's work. Acronyms are best restricted to those so widely used in the field that a key is hardly needed (for example: *FHL* for the Family History Library at Salt Lake City, *NGS* for the National Genealogical Society, *NA* or *NARA* for the National Archives, and *TAG* for *The American Genealogist*). Each acronym should be fully identified the first time it appears. If numerous acronyms are considered essential, a key should be added to the front of the manuscript or publication.

- *Referring readers to another note in which the actual reference is given* (example: when note 72 reads "see note 49"). Source notes are distracting in the first place. Readers must break their train of thought to search for the note. Being sent to yet another location simply because the writer did not want to retype the source is an annoyance that causes many readers to ignore citations altogether.

Worse, the diligent reader who does follow the chain of citations to another note often finds that it does not match the text statement that launched the search, because of one danger inherent in this kind of citation. Writers revise their early drafts. They add, delete, or rearrange information—sometimes forgetting to adjust the corresponding notes. Modern word-processing programs alter note numbers automatically to save writers a dreary chore. But when the text of a reference note reads "see note 49" and note 49 is renumbered to become 51, the internal mention of note 49 will not be automatically updated by most word-processing software.

SOURCE NOTES FOR NARRATIVE ACCOUNTS
CAN BE PRESENTED IN FOUR WAYS
- FOOTNOTES
- ENDNOTES
- PARENTHETICAL CITATIONS
- HYPERTEXT

The first three formats are traditional; the last is a recent innovation for electronic publishing. All four options are not of equal merit. Among the traditional three, footnotes (source citations and explanations appearing at the foot of each page) and endnotes (those appearing at the end of a section of text) are the recommended forms for genealogists and other historical researchers. The practice of placing source notes in parentheses within the text was once popular among genealogists and is still widely used in some other fields. However, it has been discarded by the major genealogical journals because it hampers full citations, limits crucial source discussions, and disrupts the train of thought in the narrative.

Whether we choose footnotes or endnotes is a matter of personal or editorial choice. However, footnotes have two advantages. They are easier on the reader, and photocopied pages will include automatically the source notes that correspond to the text.

Hypertext is an electronic option for those who publish digital documents that support it. A "mechanical" shortcut, hypertext involves the special highlighting of specific spots in the narrative. A mouse click on the highlighting jumps the viewer to the source note, author's comment, relevant figure, appendix, or even a digital copy of the actual source. However, when digital files containing hypertext are downloaded and printed, the hypertext links are lost; thus the documentation is lost. Undoubtedly, progressive software producers will remedy this problem in the future. Meanwhile, good genealogists rarely use this feature for reporting their research.

SOURCE NOTES KEYED TO NARRATIVE TEXT
SHOULD BE NUMBERED CONSECUTIVELY; THE
CORRESPONDING NUMBERS SHOULD APPEAR
IN CORRECT SEQUENCE WITHIN THE TEXT

The once-common practice of preparing a numbered bibliography, and then numbering text statements to refer to items on that list, is a sure ticket to error and confusion. Commonly, a given item on that list is the source of various statements throughout the text; and that listed item cites all page numbers on which useful information appears. This generic approach does not tell the reader *which page* of the listed item supports *which specific statement* in the text—as proper reference notes should. Too, when sources are not cited in strict numerical sequence, it is more likely that the writer will not spot an accidentally dropped reference number.

As a general rule in expository writing, note numbers within the text are placed at the end of sentences, outside the closing punctuation mark. However, genealogists are more particular in at least two cases:

- If a sentence contains information from more than one source, it may be desirable to note each source individually—placing the first reference number at the point where the data from that source actually ends. (See figure 3, reference numbers 2 and 3.)

- If a sentence contains not only information from a source but also our personal interpretation or observations, it is best to place the reference note at the point where the source's data end and our amplification begins.

FIGURE 3

lacement of note numbers . . . .

TEXT AND CORRESPONDING FOOTNOTES:

John*¹* Jones, the earliest-known progenitor of our family, was born about 1837 in Glasgow, Scotland.[1] On 7 December 1870 he married Mary Smith,[2] possibly in Middleville, Missouri, where he operated a shoe shop at the time of that year's census.[3] John and Mary remained . . .

---

1. John Jones, declaration of intention, 27 July 1873, Any County Naturalization Book 3: 25, Circuit Clerk's Office, Countyseat, Missouri.

2. Mary (Smith) Jones Diary, owned in 1996 by her great-granddaughter, Merry Schmit James (111 First Street; Middleville, MO 00000).

3. 1870 U.S. census, Any County, Missouri, population schedule, village of Middleville, page 2, dwelling 23, family 24; National Archives (NA) micropublication M0000, roll 000. 1870 U.S. census, Any County, Missouri, industrial schedule, Middleville, page 1, line 27; NA T000, roll 00.

In the text above, the superscript number following the name John *denotes generation number. It appears in italics to distinguish it from the note number. Some numbering systems use other conventions to make this distinction between generation number and note number.*

In both cases, the source number should appear immediately after the punctuation mark that divides the two parts of the sentence. *A source number should never appear directly after a given name, unless there is intervening punctuation,* because the superscript position immediately after a given name is the place genealogy reserves for an individual's generation number. (See John[1] in figure 3.)

EXPLICIT SOURCE NOTES SHOULD ALSO APPEAR ON ANCESTOR CHARTS AND FAMILY GROUP SHEETS

Point 1 (page 19) applies as much to family group sheets and ancestor charts as it does to any other type of genealogical compilation: any statement of fact that is not common knowledge must carry its own individual statement of source.

The practice of appending to a group sheet (or chart) a generic list of thirty-nine sources from which that sheet's ninety-two names, dates, and places have been extracted is no longer acceptable. No piece of data on that sheet can be evaluated—its reliability cannot be judged—unless its source is identified. Forcing oneself or others to comb dozens of references to identify the origin of one item of information is a needless waste.[1]

Point 7 goes one step further: when conflicting data exist for a single date, event, or relationship—and the discrepancy has not been resolved—the chart or the group sheet should record and separately document each piece of conflicting data. Arbitrarily choosing one fact over another in order to fit something into the limited space on

---

1. Note, however, that the sequential numbering which point 6 recommends for narrative text is impractical for data accumulated on group sheets and charts. Both of these items are "working documents" on which data are added in a random pattern as new information is found.

a form, while relegating conflicting data to notes in another location, is a common cause of research problems.

Genealogists who depend upon computer programs to compile their group sheets and charts should choose their program carefully, with an eye toward documentation capability. Major software programs today permit varying degrees of documentation on group sheets; but even the best of these (to this writer's knowledge) still force the genealogist to convert ancestor charts into graphics, to which another program can add the necessary note numbers and supporting documentation.

FULL CITATIONS SHOULD BE AFFIXED TO THE FRONT SIDE OF EVERY PHOTOCOPIED DOCUMENT AND SHOULD APPEAR ON EVERY PAGE OF A RESEARCH REPORT

Researchers who overlook this caution cause themselves and others much unnecessary grief. No one wishes to mar or alter the face of a document, nor should they. Consequently, many careful researchers routinely pen documentation on the reverse. As that photocopy goes into circulation, the inevitable happens: someone in the circulation chain fails to copy the back side of the record. Thereafter, no one who receives it will know its source. Penning or typing the documentation into margin space on the photocopy's front side will prevent this problem. If adequate margin does not exist, it is usually possible to use the photocopier's reduction feature to allow enough margin for source citation.

Similar problems occur when researchers type their research notes or format those entered on-site in a notebook computer. It does not suffice to identify the repository on the first page only of the report or—when an abstract runs onto a second page—to identify the abstract only at its beginning. Once the notes are reduced to hard copy, those sheets of paper will inevitably become shuffled and individual sheets will stray into other files. If the data remain in electronic form, the cut-and-paste procedures used in reorganization will separate one note from another, and the notes that lack full documentation will then become mystery objects that frustrate us every time we encounter them.

WE SHOULD NOT CITE SOURCES WE HAVE NOT USED; IT IS BOTH RISKY AND UNETHICAL TO "BORROW NOTES" FROM OTHER WRITERS

As genealogists, we have all heard that original sources are preferable to copies, extracts, or interpretative works. Therein lies a sinkhole in which we can easily flounder. When we use a published source or other derivative work, if the author provides a citation to an original document (or any other source), it is neither safe nor ethical for us to cite the other unless we actually consult it. We must cite what we use, and credit should always be given where it is due. By the same token, we would not wish to inherit the blame for an error another writer made when using a record we have not seen.

An acceptable practice for us would ordinarily be one or both of the following:

- Record the detail as it appears in the published source; identify that source fully; then note that the writer cites his or her source as ... [*here we copy the citation exactly—as on page 45, note 1*].

- Consult the cited material to verify that the writer has reported the information correctly and to determine whether there is additional information to be gleaned.

If the published source cites an original record, we should indeed follow the second option: examine the original and cite it as our own reference. If the secondary work has given us special insight

29

into the use or interpretation of the original, we should also credit the secondary source for this insight. If the original material is of a nature that we might not have found on our own, we may also wish to credit the secondary work for calling this material to our attention. If, on the other hand, the secondary work erroneously reports the facts from the original, then that error should be explained in a discussion added to our source note.

EVEN A FULL CITATION OF SOURCE MAY NOT BE SUFFICIENT, LEGALLY OR ETHICALLY, WHEN COPYING FROM ANOTHER WORK

Crediting other authors, or properly citing the whereabouts of specific documents, may not be adequate protection for us if we publish. The issues of copyright, plagiarism, and fair use also come into play. There are ambiguous limits to the amount of material we can quote from another source. Some publishers require permission—as well as acknowledgment in our citation—if more than three hundred or so words are copied. Some set other limits. The following rules of thumb are reasonably safe guidelines:

- When copying more than *three words* from another source, we treat those words as a quote. (If the material is short—three lines or less—we weave the quote into our text, setting it off with quotation marks. If the material is longer, we set it off in an indented paragraph, without quotation marks.) The source of the quote should be clearly identified. The use of another person's words, thoughts, or material without giving them credit is *plagiarism.*

- When using more than *three paragraphs* from another source, we obtain permission from the author and the publisher. If permission is granted, our credit line acknowledges that permission.

- When quoting from *manuscript material* owned by an individual, agency, or institution, we also seek permission. Some archives severely limit copying, quoting, or publishing from their collections.

In applying these guidelines, we should also consider two other questions that relate to the principle of *fair use:*

- What is the proportion of our copied material in comparison to the body of information from which we have taken that material? Court decisions rarely uphold reuse of more than a small fraction of the whole.

- Will we market our work in competition against the individual or agency whose work we have merged into our own? If so, our reuse would not be fair use at all.

MICROFORMS AND ELECTRONIC
MATERIALS NEED EXTRA TREATMENT

Proper source citation has been greatly complicated by the emergence of microfilm, microfiche, and electronic media as modes of publication. The range of materials produced in these formats almost defies standardization. When we examine a publication and attempt to define the elements that need recording, we should keep in mind that this material commonly has two descriptive parts:

- Most such material *originated in manuscript or book form*. It may have been created in modern times or it may be antiquated data.

- Most such material is *now being published by a firm or an agency* that is not the original creator.

Therefore, the citation we record should

- distinguish between duplicated records and information arranged in a database;

- credit properly the original creator;

- credit properly the producer of the film or electronic publication;

- identify thoroughly the nature of the material that is being used;

31

- identify the film or electronic publication completely enough for others to locate it;

- cite the specific place (page, frame, etc.) on the roll, fiche, or database at which we found the relevant detail; and

- cite the date on which the micropublication or electronic data set was created, as well as the date of the relevant record.

As a generic example, an electronic database may be billed as an index to all marriages within a state. Superficially, it might seem sufficient to cite the work in the following manner:

> *Marriages in Anystate,* CD-ROM Disc 111
> (Anycity: Eureka Corporation, 1996).

That citation may suffice for us or anyone else to obtain the CD and verify the accuracy of the transcription we made from that particular CD. Yet that citation is *not* sufficient to permit us or anyone else to make a judgment about the reliability of the CD's information. Where did Eureka Corporation get its database?

If the publisher has thoughtfully provided a preface stating that it bought its data from another firm or individual, is that detail sufficient to our needs? No. To analyze validity, we also need to know

- the identity of the *original* creator—the human being—who first compiled that data set;

- the source(s) from which the data were taken; and

- whether the database represents full or partial extraction from those sources or whether it was generated from materials randomly encountered by the original compiler.

It can be difficult to track the origins of material of this type—especially if the publisher does not recognize the value of proper source citation. A currently marketed database may have been purchased from a firm no longer in existence, which may have bought its data from a book compiler, who may have assembled his or her marriage lists from random records abstracted in genealogical society magazines. Such a database would be an entirely different creature from one issued by—let us say—a state society using carefully selected volunteers in each county to extract every marriage record known to be extant for their respective regions.

What if our efforts to track the origin of the material are unsuccessful? Our note should say so and explain the effort we made. This will help us and other researchers avoid unnecessary repetition of the same efforts. And, with time, we or a correspondent or a reader may find a hole that can be plugged in our discovery process—if we have carefully recorded the steps we have taken.

Microfilmed materials can present other problems. Two resources that require special attention are those of the Family History Library (FHL) in Salt Lake City and the National Archives (NA) in Washington.

Family History Library Microforms

The trove of microfilm and fiche available at the Family History Library of the Church of Jesus Christ of Latter-day Saints is so varied that additional considerations are needed to construct a clear citation:

- Records of local, state, and federal governments held by the library in microform are commonly cited in the same manner as those records would be in their original depositories—by copying the label precisely from the filmed book or file, rather than by copying the FHL label.

- When using an FHL copy of a National Archives microfilm, we should identify (from the beginning of the roll) the name and publication number of the NA production, as well as the roll number within that production. (Example: M279, *Records of the 1820 Census of Manufactures,* roll 13.)

- It is also wise (but not obligatory) to add a notation that the FHL film was used. Sometimes the FHL edition differs from film editions of the same record elsewhere, and any film edition could omit pages found in the original.

• Recording the FHL call number in our notes can be helpful to us later in our own research. However, we will create problems if we (*a*) record *only* the FHL call number; or (*b*) append FHL's number to our citation of an original record without explicitly identifying that number as FHL cataloging. Other libraries that hold that same film will invariably have their own call numbers.

• Books and privately created manuscripts held by FHL in microform should be cited as the original book or manuscript would be cited. Again, we may wish to add the appropriate FHL call number, identifying it as such. Because items of this type seldom use a full roll of film and other items appear on the same roll, we will also want to record the *internal item number* that FHL has assigned to the specific material we studied on that roll.

• Ancestor charts, family group sheets, temple-work submissions, and similarly compiled materials should carry full identification of the compiler of the individual record. In this case, we should definitely record the FHL call number and cite FHL as the repository, because the material is unique to that facility.

See part 2 of this manual for specific citation formats for these and other FHL materials.

National Archives Microforms

This facility offers a style guide for researchers (see bibliography), illustrating its preferred manner of citing its resources. However, the extreme length of most recommended forms makes them burdensome in compilations that are heavily laced with National Archives material. (This has been a standard complaint against Lackey's *Cite Your Sources*, which closely followed NA guidelines.) The Archives' own journal, *Prologue,* applies a more concise citation style—although some of that journal's citation forms (particularly for census data) are not explicit enough to meet genealogical needs.

A compromise seems sensible. The most problematic area of NA's style manual is its treatment of microform, which not only records a full citation for the publication data but also adds a full citation for the original records from which the film was made. Most careful genealogists simply cite one or the other—films or originals—depending upon which was consulted. The practice is soundly grounded, because a citation should make it clear *exactly* what material we consult.

Electronic publishing online and the imaging and informal transmission of data online are increasingly important to family historians. Their roles in reliable research and the extent to which this type of material can be preserved as a permanent record are issues that are still debatable and fluid. Part 2 offers citation formats that are only basic and temporary. Alterations and amplifications will be necessary as electronic publication continues to develop.

CLEAR CITATIONS REQUIRE
ATTENTION TO MANY DETAILS

Mies van der Rohe once declared, "God is in the details!" He spoke of the building blocks of architecture, not those of source citation; but his observation still applies. Beyond the main points covered in this chapter, a variety of other details contributes to a clear format for recording and reporting our references.

Correct bibliographic data

The title page should be consulted to identify a book's name properly. Spines and covers often carry shortened versions. If the work is no longer at hand when we realize that we need additional publication data, we can seek an accurate bibliographic entry from the Library of Congress's ongoing series *National Union Catalog*—available in the reference department of major libraries—or the OCLC (On-line Computer Library Center) electronic database that librarians conventionally use, or consult the Library of Congress web site.

Latin "shorthand"

Latin terms are rarely seen today as a means of shortening reference citations. *Op cit., supra, infra,* and *cf.* are now obsolete idioms few researchers can even define. Two others are holdovers: *sic* (which means "There's an error here that I'm copying exactly, but I'm pointing it out so you won't think the error is mine") and *ibid.* Several particulars need to be borne in mind when using the latter:

- *Ibid.* means "in the same source as above."

- *Ibid.* is not used if the prior note cites multiple references.

- *Ibid.* is not used if the prior note has discursive text as well as a citation of the source.

- *Ibid.* is not used until the final manuscript is prepared. When used in preliminary drafts, a rearrangement of text or notes can separate an *ibid.* from the preceding note to which it belongs. Thereafter, the citation represented by that *ibid.* would be incorrect.

Capitalization

Capitalization of titles varies according to circumstances. It is useful to remember the following:

- Setting a title entirely in capital letters is frowned upon—an offense to typography because it crowds the lines of type and visually overwhelms. Instead, book titles should be italicized (see Stylistic Tips, figure 5) or underlined.

- When typing online (i.e., over an electronic network) or storing data in ASCII computer files, limitations there may require an exception to the above rule. Capitalization is recommended as a substitute for italics whenever italics cannot be generated by the electronic system in use.

- English titles capitalize all words except articles (except when used as first word of title or subtitle), coordinating conjunctions, and prepositions. German titles capitalize only nouns. In some foreign languages, it is customary to capitalize only proper nouns and the first word of a title, regardless of its length. (As an exception: American library catalogers generally capitalize only the first word, a practice that has not been accepted by most style manuals for writing and publishing.)

- If the title page of a book uses incorrect capitalization, it is permissible to correct the usage in our citations. We cannot change the words of the title, but we can properly capitalize them.

Punctuation

If the title of a book or article ignores punctuation conventions or omits diacritical marks, it is permissible to correct the problem. If we do not, our own readers will assume *we* have committed the offense.

Defining "published" material

Many rules of citation require us to distinguish between published and unpublished material. However, these lines are continually blurring as new media develop. As a rule of thumb at present:

- *Published* material may be defined as material that is photocopied, put into microform, reduced to electronic disks, or placed online with the intent to disseminate it widely.

- *Unpublished* material may exist in these same forms but may have been produced only for preservation or for very limited sharing.

To illustrate: a set of estate papers in a given courthouse may exist in these varied forms:

Original loose papers . . . . unpublished

Original manuscript volumes . . . . unpublished

Microfilmed copies of the loose papers,
    supplied to a state archives without
    permission to rent or sell copies . . . . unpublished

Microfilmed copies of the bound volumes,
    made with the intent to rent or sell . . . . published

REMEMBER:

CITING A SOURCE IS NOT AN END TO ITSELF;
OUR REAL GOAL IS TO HAVE THE
BEST POSSIBLE SOURCE TO CITE

In the research stage, we will want to record every source consulted, regardless of our opinion of its value—but we cannot be content just to cite *something*. When we recognize that a source is deficient or that a better source should exist, the better source should be sought and used. When we convert our raw notes into an interpretative account, we will want our data and our conclusions to be supported by sound evidence of the highest quality possible. That is the subject explored in the next chapter.

FIGURE 4

*A*bbreviation tips . . . .

STANDARD ABBREVIATIONS:

assn.	= *association*	n.p.	=	*no publisher shown*
bk.	= *book*			*no publication place*
chap.	= *chapter*	N.S.	=	*new series, new style*
Co.	= *County, Company*	O.S.	=	*Old series, Old style*
col.	= *column*	pt.	=	*part*
comp.	= *compiler*	p./pp.	=	*page(s)*
c./ca.	= *circa*	p.p.	=	*privately printed*
dept.	= *department*	rev. ed.	=	*revised edition*
ed.	= *edition, editor*	RG	=	*record group*
eds.	= *editors*	sect.	=	*section*
et al.	= *and others*	ser.	=	*series*
fo.	= *folio*	supp.	=	*supplement*
ff.	= *and following*	transcr.	=	*transcriber*
MS/MSS	= *manuscript(s)*	transl.	–	*translator*
no.	= *number*	v./vs.	=	*versus*
n./nn.	= *note(s)*	ver.	=	*version*
n.d.	= *no publication date*	vol.	=	*volume*

OTHER CONSIDERATIONS:

1. State names are shortened in two ways:
    *   Two-letter postal codes are used for mailing addresses.
    *   Standard abbreviations are preferred in all other contexts.
2. Page numbers need not be preceded by "p." when citing books and articles. When citing censuses, newspapers, or other records that may involve references to several types of numbers (e.g., p. 37, dwelling 245, family 246; or p. 3, col. 2), the inclusion of "p." before the page number will usually help to clarify the citation.
3. Abbreviated credentials (postnomials) following personal names are often punctuated differently according to type.
    *   Academic credentials are usually punctuated with periods.
    *   Professional credentials are often written as acronyms, with no periods. (See also appendix.)
4. Abbreviations do not save a significant amount of space. The thoughtful writer avoids all but the truly obvious.

FIGURE 5

*S*tylistic tips
for source notes . . . .

1. *Italics,* used in the name of a source, signify that it is a
   * court case (or)
   * publication (book, CD-ROM, fiche, film, journal, or map).
   Names of unpublished works, other than court cases, should
   not be italicized.

2. *Quotation marks,* used around the name of a source, signify
   * a manuscript, dissertation, or thesis that is unpublished (or)
   * an article within a journal (or)
   * a chapter within a book.
   Although newspapers put quotation marks around book
   names, that practice generally is not followed elsewhere.

3. *Ellipses* (three dots, with spaces before, between, and after)
   signify that part of the original title is deleted.

4. *Square brackets* [ ] are used to signify that the editor or transcriber has added words not found in the original source. Parentheses should not be substituted.

5. *Angle brackets* < > are used around electronic addresses.

6. *Capitalization* should be limited to proper nouns. It is not
   necessary to capitalize *volume, book, roll, census,* or other
   similar words, unless they are part of a formal title that appears in quotation marks or italics.

7. *Postnomials* (initials appearing after the name to indicate professional credentials and academic degrees) are written in capi-
   tals that are reduced in size to the height of the *x* in the font
   being used. Academic degrees traditionally are punctuated
   with periods. Professional credentials may be written as acronyms, without periods. Credentials outside the field are not
   normally cited unless they relate to the genealogical subject
   on which the author writes (e.g.: an M.D. who writes on genetics). For more on credentials, see the appendix.

FIGURE 6

ibliographic tips . . . .

WHEN COMPILING A LIST OF SOURCES:

1. Apply the guidelines found under Stylistic Tips, figure 5.

2. Subdivide the list into at least two categories: "original sources" and "derivative works." (See next chapter's discussion of this subject.)

3. List works in alphabetical order, by author, within each section. If no author is known for a particular work, the title becomes the first cited element and its first word determines its alphabetic placement.

4. Group together all works by the same author.

5. For authors of multiple works, don't repeat the author's name in each listing. It is given fully in the first instance; subsequent items use a 3-em dash (i.e., a dash whose length corresponds to three times the width of our font's *m*) in place of the author's name. If em dashes are not available in our software or if we are using a typewriter, an underscore of that same length may be substituted.

6. If an author produced some works alone and some with other writers, first group all those produced alone, and then group all those published under joint authorship, listing them thereunder alphabetically by the names of the second authors. Again, we use a 3-em dash instead of repeating the primary author's name.

7. Do not number bibliographic items.

Exception to number 7:
When preparing handouts or syllabus material for a lecture, the bibliographic items should be numbered for easy reference during the lecture.

$\mathcal{F}$undamentals of analysis . . . .

Genealogy is a study to which most people come after they have already mastered other fields. Many of these—history and other social sciences, the physical and biological sciences, law, and journalism, as examples—are rooted in research and analysis.

Yet the special nature of genealogical conclusions often requires us to modify research principles used elsewhere before we can successfully apply them to our genealogical problems. In genealogy, there is a more rigorous standard than those common in the social sciences, where individual oversights or errors tend to cancel each other out in the broad perspective—or those in the hard sciences, where experiments will expose errors. In genealogy, a single wrong relationship is multiplied exponentially with each generation beyond the error.

Careful analysis of evidence may even require us to alter the processes by which our basic knowledge was acquired. Many school systems still emphasize rote learning of facts from selected textbooks. Many students still are not taught to question the correctness of the facts and opinions therein. Many Americans still grow to adulthood believing in the integrity of the printed word, trusting the research of published "experts." Much academic research in the humanities is still conducted more in published sources than in the raw stuff of history, inconveniently housed in courthouse attics and obscure archives.

Genealogical research—done well—requires a critical approach to knowledge. Answers to questions can seldom be "looked up" in books. Even when we find needed answers there, they often contradict each other. If no conflict is apparent, we are still expected to verify those published facts. Documents are just as suspect; we persistently question the motive and the knowledge of their creators.

Are we cynical? No, just cautious. As researchers, we do not speculate; we test. We critically observe and carefully record. Then we must weigh the accumulated evidence—analyzing the individual parts as well as the whole, without favoring any theory. Bias, ego, patronage, prejudice, pride, or shame cannot tinge our decisions when we appraise our evidence.

Above all, we must remember that historical and genealogical truths are elusive. Prior to genetic testing, legal "proof" of relationship was more likely than not a matter of assumption and trust. All families have had situations in which a person's parentage has been debated. We cannot—a generation, a century, a half-millennium later—*prove* a relationship beyond any shadow of doubt.

Every kinship, every fact, every identity we establish is simply a decision we base upon the evidence we have accumulated. Our challenge is to accumulate the best evidence possible and to train ourselves to analyze and interpret that evidence in the most perceptive manner possible.

To help you toward that goal, this chapter surveys thirteen basic principles that good genealogists apply to the analysis of evidence.

FIGURE 7

uidelines for
analyzing evidence . . . .

1. Direct evidence is easier to understand, but indirect evidence can carry equal weight.

2. Reliable genealogical conclusions are based on the weight—not quantity—of the evidence found.

3. Evidence should be drawn from a variety of independently created sources.

4. Original source material generally is more reliable than derivative material.

5. The reliability of a derivative work is influenced by the degree of processing it has undergone.

6. The purpose of a record and the motivation of its creators frequently affect its truthfulness.

7. The most reliable informants have firsthand knowledge of the events to which they testify.

8. The veracity and skill of a record's creator will have shaped its content.

9. Timeliness generally adds to a document's credibility.

10. Penmanship can establish identity, date, and authenticity.

11. A record's custodial history affects its trustworthiness.

12. All known records should be used and a thorough effort made to identify unknown materials.

13. The case is never closed on a genealogical conclusion.

DIRECT EVIDENCE IS EASIER TO UNDERSTAND,
BUT INDIRECT EVIDENCE CAN CARRY EQUAL WEIGHT

Direct evidence is that which addresses a particular matter and points to a conclusion without the addition of other supporting evidence.

Indirect evidence is circumstantial information that requires us to supply a thought process (and perhaps other evidence) to convert its detail into a reliable conclusion.

According to genealogy's now-classic discussion by Noel C. Stevenson, J.D., FASG, "Evidence is none the less effective because it is circumstantial, if it be consistent, connected and conclusive."[1] To use indirect or circumstantial evidence effectively, though, genealogists must hone their analytic skills and expand their understanding of the strengths and limits of various source materials.

RELIABLE GENEALOGICAL CONCLUSIONS
ARE BASED ON THE WEIGHT—NOT
QUANTITY—OF EVIDENCE FOUND

Each time we accept or reject a fact or a probability, that decision should be based upon careful consideration of where the *weight* of the evidence lies. That weight is based upon the *quality* of the evidence, not upon the number of documents accumulated—although

---

1. Noel C. Stevenson, *Genealogical Evidence: A Guide to the Standard of Proof Relating to Pedigrees, Ancestry, Heirship and Family History,* revised edition (Laguna Hills, California: Aegean Park Press, 1989), 186. As his authority, Stevenson cites *"State* v. *Samuels,* 6 Pennewill's Delaware Reports 36, 39."

a reliable effort to determine "truth" or likelihood requires us to consult all known sources. As we weigh our evidence, we frequently find that it falls on both sides of the balance scale. If it does not, we should be especially sure that we have not overlooked any relevant material.

Thorough research customarily results in one of the following:

- We may uncover multiple pieces of evidence that directly state the information we need. If that evidence satisfies the other requirements discussed in this chapter, then we have a *simple accumulation of direct evidence* that strongly supports one conclusion.

- We may never find a document that states directly what we need to know, although we may find multiple pieces of quality evidence that indirectly suggest one particular solution, with no inherent contradictions. If so, then we may build a case upon *an assemblage of indirect or circumstantial evidence.*

- We may accumulate conflicting evidence—direct, indirect, or a combination of both. A *resolution of conflicting evidence* requires us to weigh each piece for credibility and resolve the contradictions in a clearly convincing manner.

Building a case when documents disagree or do not state directly what we want to know (a necessity often but imprecisely called "using the preponderance-of-evidence principle") requires a fuller understanding of how "evidence" (information found) becomes "proof" (information accepted) in legal and genealogical practice.

In theory

Modern genealogy draws heavily from law in its handling of evidence. Yet genealogy requires a higher standard of proof than does most civil litigation, and attempts to define genealogical concepts by legal terms create confusion. Consider this comparison:

- The justice system requires that a date be set for trial, that all known and valid evidence be considered at this time, and that a decision be made then and there on the basis of that evidence. To avoid clogging the court system, the law permits decisions to be made in the closest of cases—even when the evidence on one side barely outweighs that on the other. This is the legal standard of proof called *preponderance of the evidence.*

- Genealogy rarely sees an arbitrary time or deadline by which one must decide the parentage of a distant forebear. If clearly convincing evidence does not exist to accept or reject a point, the genealogist can—and should—simply delay a decision until suitable evidence is found.[2]

In practice

As careful genealogists, when we thoroughly exhaust all potential resources, we will carefully analyze each element and apply at least the points set forth in this chapter. If the weight of the evidence suggests a reasonable conclusion, we will labor to disprove our hypothesis as diligently as we labor to prove it. When we find contrary evidence, we will adequately and logically rebut it—or else delay our decision until clearer support can be assembled. When we are convinced that all valid evidence points to a conclusion that we and others of experience and rational thinking can accept as clearly convincing, then we may be ready to present our case.

To argue a case—whether upon an *assemblage of circumstantial evidence* or a *resolution of conflicting evidence*—we must reduce our argument to paper. The object is a clearly written, logically reasoned, totally documented summary of the problem, the records consulted, the methodology used, the evidence found, and the conclusion we believe is justified.

---

2. A legal term sometimes applied—*clear and convincing proof*—is also problematic for genealogy, because its legal interpretation varies between jurisdictions. Some equate it with *beyond a reasonable doubt* (the standard for criminal cases), while others treat it as an intermediate standard between "no reasonable doubt" and a simple "preponderance." See Henry Campbell Black, *Black's Law Dictionary,* 5th edition, Joseph R. Nolan and M. J. Connolly, editors (Saint Paul, Minnesota: West Publishing Co., 1979), 147 ("beyond a reasonable doubt"), 227 ("clear and convincing proof"), and 1064 ("preponderance of evidence").

EVIDENCE SHOULD BE
DRAWN FROM A VARIETY OF
INDEPENDENTLY CREATED SOURCES

It is sometimes argued, simplistically, that a point is "proved" only if we have three, four, or five sources that report the same fact. But there is no magic number. The crucial issues are the reliability of the sources, the origins of their information, and the thoroughness with which we use all the available material.

If we are fortunate to find more than one source that states a specific fact we need, we must then ask a question: are those sources *independently created?* If fraudulent testimony is given in a court case in 1742, and then a nineteenth-century writer reports the details of that case in a local history, and a twentieth-century genealogist repeats the account without documentation, we have three "quite different" sources that state the same facts. Does that *prove* the facts? No. We do not have three *independently created* sources that coincidentally verify each other. We have one bad piece of information that has been perpetuated.

ORIGINAL SOURCE MATERIAL GENERALLY IS
MORE RELIABLE THAN DERIVATIVE MATERIAL

Those who study the course of human events traditionally classify evidence as *primary* and *secondary.*[3] Genealogists have done the same. However, trying to force our evidence into one category or the other is frequently an exercise in futility and frustration.

---

3. As a highly abbreviated definition of primary and secondary evidence: *primary* refers to original material; *secondary* to all else. Between these extremes are countless materials that defy a clear assignment to either.

A far better gauge is to appraise our evidence in terms of *original material* and *derivative material.*

Original material, as defined by the purist, is based on firsthand knowledge—be it oral or written. It is the testimony of a person relating events that he or she personally experienced or witnessed. It is an original document created by a party with firsthand knowledge of the information being recorded.

Derivative material is all else. Its weight can span the entire spectrum of reliability—depending upon the form that it takes, the circumstances of its creation, and the skill and reliability of its creator. A debatable hierarchy for appraising derivative material might be

- *Duplicates:* As defined by *Federal Civil Judicial Procedure and Rules* (see bibliography), Rule 1002 (4), a duplicate is "a counterpart produced by the same impression as the original, or from the same matrix, or by means of photography, including enlargements and miniatures or by mechanical or electrical rerecording, or by chemical reproduction or by other equivalent techniques which accurately reproduce the original."

  Rule 1003 of the same code addresses the acceptability of duplicates. In courts of law, under most circumstances, a duplicate is as admissible as the original would be. However, the presenter of a duplicate is obligated to explain why it is presented in lieu of the original.

  Duplicates are a staple of genealogical research. Official and business correspondence prior to the mid-twentieth century used letterpress and carbon processes to produce file copies. More recently, photographic reproduction and digitized images have facilitated our access to remote records. In many cases, the duplicate may be the only surviving copy. In other instances, it may be the only one to which we have access. In any event, the reliability of a duplicate is influenced by all the factors discussed in points 5 through 11 of this chapter.

- *Transcripts:* These verbatim copies, manuscript or typed, attempt to render the words and punctuation just as the original scribe presented them. Transcripts are also a common source for genealogists who pride themselves on doing research in the "best possible" material. Documents found in the record books of town and county clerks are commonly transcripts made from original papers presented to the clerk for recording. Rarely have the originals survived. Those record books themselves may be transcripts of older volumes that have distintegrated. Census marshals of the past often transcribed additional copies for submission to multiple offices. Such transcripts often are the best possible sources that remain today.

- *Edited transcripts:* These more-or-less verbatim copies, usually published, typically apply a variety of editorial conventions ranging from correction of punctuation, grammar, and spelling to augmentation of facts. Published diaries, memoirs, and presidential papers are common examples that blur the traditional lines between "best" and "second-best" evidence. The "originals" themselves may or may not meet the other tests applied in points 5 through 11. Likewise, the edited transcripts may be more or less trustworthy, depending upon the integrity and skill of the editor.

Beyond this point, derivative works take many forms that often are of less reliability:

- *Abstracts:* abbreviated summaries of documents.

- *Extracts:* verbatim transcripts of selected portions of documents.

- *Compendiums:* compilations of data gleaned from an assortment of related materials.

- *Histories, genealogies, and expository essays:* narrative accounts, supposedly based on facts taken from assorted records that the author has analyzed and reported in terms of his or her own interpretation. (Potential reliability is commonly judged by the degree to which compilers document each statement of fact with a reliable source.)

- *Traditions:* family or legendary accounts passed down through the generations.

THE RELIABILITY OF A DERIVATIVE WORK
IS INFLUENCED BY THE DEGREE OF
PROCESSING IT HAS UNDERGONE

As careful researchers, we also consider the *amount* of processing our information has undergone. A derivative work may be one or several steps removed from the original. A deed book in the town clerk's office could be a record copy of the original documents or it could be a third-generation copy made when the first record book became timeworn. As cautious genealogists, we will also examine the inside covers and the initial and closing pages of each record book, for a clerical notation that the book has been recopied.

Each additional layer of processing adds the likelihood of transcription errors. The rank, post, title, or education of the individual who transformed the data can increase or reduce the *likelihood* of error, but it does not change the fact that each mutation is likely to be less accurate than the parent copy. Thus, we diligently track the ancestry of derivative works, hoping to trace each to its original source—at the least, to the earliest extant version.

THE PURPOSE OF A RECORD AND
THE MOTIVATION OF ITS CREATORS
FREQUENTLY AFFECT ITS TRUTHFULNESS

Many documents are created for self-serving purposes, and all are produced by individuals of varying degrees of reliability. As careful genealogists, we can take no record at face value. In appraising various types of materials, we apply such tests as the following two:

- *Affidavits or other sworn statements* (for a legal case, pension application, or damage claim): To what extent did the complainants, defendants, or witnesses have cause for bias or gain?

- *Bible or diary:* To what extent might the creator have had cause to misrepresent a fact? For example: a backdated marriage in the family bible to hide a firstborn's premature birth; or a diary entry that exaggerates the writer's role in an event because he or she anticipates that the diary will be made public.

THE MOST RELIABLE INFORMANTS HAVE
FIRSTHAND KNOWLEDGE OF THE
EVENTS TO WHICH THEY TESTIFY

Death certificates provide a classic example for illustrating the point. The informant for a death certificate, let us say, is the spouse of the deceased. We may logically expect the surviving spouse to have firsthand knowledge of the decedent's address, identity, and occupation. We would not expect the spouse to have firsthand knowledge of the decedent's birth, because it is improbable that the spouse was present at that birth; the spouse's knowledge of the person's birth date might be more accurately termed *hearsay*. On the other hand, the spouse's knowledge of the identity of the decedent's parents could be firsthand, if the spouse knew them personally.

THE VERACITY AND SKILL OF A RECORD'S
CREATOR WILL HAVE SHAPED ITS CONTENT

Appraising this factor can be one of the most difficult tasks that the genealogist undertakes. It asks that we not only study the information inherent in a record but also acquaint ourselves with the scribe who penned the original document and any compiler(s) who prepared derivative works that we consult. For example:

- *Local government records:* Does the court clerk's other work exhibit signs of care or carelessness? Might he be an unqualified or uninterested political appointee? Case in point: Lew Wallace, famed as a Civil War general and author of *Ben Hur,* was a lackadaisical, fifteen-year-old school dropout—and son of the state governor— when he was appointed assistant clerk of Marion County, Indiana. His assignment: copying deeds and judgments at ten cents per hundred words.[4] Meticulously recorded documents from that place and time should not be expected.

- *Published records or genealogies:* How experienced is the preparer? What is his or her reputation as a genealogist? For this reason, among others, good references go beyond the cryptic notation of just *journal/issue/page*. The identity of the person who contributed the information to that publication can add or subtract weight when we appraise the publication's value.

TIMELINESS GENERALLY ADDS TO
A DOCUMENT'S CREDIBILITY

Did months or years elapse between the event and the creation of the record that relates its details? As a general rule of thumb (which may or may not be correct in any given case), a record that is created closer to the time of the event is more credible than one created long after. Typical of the questions we apply in this regard are the following two:

---

4. W. H. L. Wallace, *Lew Wallace: An Autobiography,* 2 volumes (New York: Harper and Brothers, 1906), 1: chapters 7–8.

- *Affidavit for a court case or pension application:* Was the testimony taken promptly after the event or many years removed?

- *Bible record:* What is the bible's publication date? Is that date compatible with the first entry of family data, or does it appear that someone entered events from earlier years or generations? Are the ink and penmanship consistent throughout all the entries (an indication that they may have been made in one sitting), or are the entries recorded in hands of varying style and steadiness (an indication that they may have been recorded, as they occurred, over the life span of one person or over several life spans)?

PENMANSHIP CAN ESTABLISH
IDENTITY, DATE, AND AUTHENTICITY

Being able to read the penmanship found in historic documents is a basic skill for genealogists, but a sound *analysis* of penmanship goes far beyond a mere reading of the words. The manner in which letters are formed can be a distinctive characteristic of a particular ancestor, as well as a particular style of writing that the ancestor and/or his scribe was taught and the types of pen and ink that were popular at the time the document was created.

Records that seem relevant to a research problem should be evaluated from at least two standpoints:

Ancestral penmanship

For various reasons, individuals do authorize others to draft and/or sign documents in their names. Yet as careful genealogists, when we research literate ancestors or those who made distinctive marks, we try to accumulate as many examples as possible of the manner in which they put pen to paper. Then we closely compare those instances. Aberrations between signatures or marks on documents that bear the same name must be logically explained, with supporting evidence, if we assert that all these documents were created by the same individual.

Scribal penmanship

Similarly, we appraise the handwriting used elsewhere within the record book or collection that contains the relevant document. For example, a church register that appears to be an original could be an administrative copy. So we ask:

- Is the penmanship of a style common to the era in which the events occurred?

- Are all entries made in the same hand, or are there the variances one would expect from data entered over many months or years?

- Are original signatures appended to marriages and baptisms, as is common with many sacramental registers of past centuries?

- Are the entries recorded in a "form type" book for a period in which such books were not the rule? Many preprinted registers discreetly carry publication dates that may reveal their creation long after the original events occurred.

A RECORD'S CUSTODIAL HISTORY
AFFECTS ITS TRUSTWORTHINESS

The annals of history are rife with cases of forged documents, created long after the fact by someone with questionable intent. Affidavits, bible records, deeds, marriage bonds, and wills—these and more have been forged by people who wished to "prove" the unprovable.

Protecting ourselves against deliberate fraud requires us to question each document we acquire: Is it in proper custody? Was it out of that custody at any time in its past? A photocopied "document" that *should* be on public record but cannot be found is always suspect until proved otherwise—a point that underscores the need for all manuscript materials to be properly cited by name, book, page, file, collection, and repository.

As careful genealogists, we also will consider the fact that even proper custody is no guarantee of authenticity or accuracy. Numerous instances exist of forged documents that have been filed legally, of spurious papers illegally inserted into legal files long after the fact, and of baseborn alterations made to record books.

Modern technology has increased both the necessity and the difficulty of analyzing a document's authenticity. Sophisticated electronic tools permit the production of fake records of remarkable semblance to time-weathered materials. Enterprising firms and individuals are "re-creating" ship rolls and other family records for display in a fashion that appears to be original. Just as easily, the unscrupulous can add, to those redesigned rolls, passengers who never saw the ship; couples can be posed together in photographs who, in real life, were never joined by marriage, kinship, or even acquaintance. Microfilming obscures many characteristics that might, on the original document, give away fraud—a correction in mismatched ink or paper inappropriate for the era of the "record" penned upon it.

ALL KNOWN RECORDS SHOULD BE USED AND
A THOROUGH EFFORT MADE TO IDENTIFY
UNKNOWN MATERIALS

A reliable analysis cannot be made from partial evidence. Any pertinent record or collection or repository that goes unconsulted is a silent bomb waiting to explode our premature theories. The risk is great enough when, in a run of luck, we are blessed with documents that all lean toward the same conclusion. The risk cannot be chanced when, as frequently happens, we have no direct evidence to support a conclusion but propose a solution based on an assemblage of circumstantial evidence.

THE CASE IS NEVER CLOSED ON
A GENEALOGICAL CONCLUSION

The reliable analysis of any piece of historical evidence is a complex process. As good genealogists, we must repeat this process endlessly, applying the principles discussed in this chapter to every piece of evidence that we find. We also recognize that no decision regarding identity, parentage, origin, or other genealogical detail can be considered definitive. Just as scientists revise their theories in the wake of new discoveries, so do genealogists and historians. Any decision we make today could be changed tomorrow by the discovery of a new record.

In sum:

As careful genealogists, we cannot apply an easy, generic label—*reliable* or *unreliable*—to any document, much less any *type* of document. We cannot assign numerical values and add up a document's score to decide whether we should trust it. Under some misleading systems that have been proposed, a dubious factoid repeated many times can seemingly outweigh an actual fact from a single, impeccably reliable source.

Instead, we must mentally appraise the credibility of *each* detail in *each* document on a *fact-by-fact, circumstance-by-circumstance* basis, considering all the factors outlined in this chapter. As we acquire a historical and social perspective of an ancestor's place and time, as we accumulate experience in evaluating the evidence we find, this phase of research becomes a less perplexing and a more fascinating and stimulating challenge.

art 2: Citation Formats

A note regarding citation styles . . . .

The models that follow are rooted in the classic guidebook *The Chicago Manual of Style* (see bibliography). *CMS,* as it is widely known, is a standard among genealogists because it is exceedingly detailed and because its citation styles fit the needs of our field better than most comprehensive guides. However, there are some crucial differences between *CMS* and the present manual— differences prompted by three factors:

- Genealogists heavily use a few types of materials that *CMS* ignores or treats scantily because they are rare to academic and commercial presses—notably the records of local governments, churches, cemeteries, and family archives.

- Genealogy requires more-detailed source information than many other fields, primarily because it must analyze historical evidence with greater precision.

- The National Archives, whose resources are fundamental to American genealogy, has its own citation styles.

Given the breadth of resources available, it is not possible to cover all variations in a manual of handbook size. For situations in which the following models do not seem to fit, please consult other guides cited in the bibliography.

FIGURE 8. BASIC PATTERNS *of* CITATION

Record sources are endlessly varied. Yet all citations are constructed from a few basic elements. The chart below itemizes seven main types of resources genealogists use and matches each to the specific elements we need to locate and appraise them.

Basic Elements   • = almost always applicable   s = sometimes applicable

Basic Elements	Archival manuscripts	Articles	Books	Censuses	Electronic data²	Local gov't. records¹	Microform²
Author's or compiler's¹ name (in full)	•	•	•		s		s
Title of book/document/disk/film	•	•	•		•	•	•
Publication place			•	•	•	•	•
Publisher's name		•	•		•	•	•
Publication date (year)		•	•		•	•	•
Publication date (month/season, year)		•			•		
Title of article, database, or film item		•			s		s
Volume number (periodicals & book sets)	•	•	•	•	s		s
Publication number (film or disk)	•	•		•	•	•	s
Page/frame/folio number	•	•	•	•	•	•	•
Document/file name	•				s	•	s
Document/file number	•				s	•	s
Collection name (if applicable)	•				s	•	s
Collection number (if applicable)	•				s	•	s
Repository name (if applicable)	•			•		•	
Repository location (if applicable)	•			•	•	•	•
Enumeration or document date	•			•		•	
Enumeration-district name/number				•		•	
Dwelling/family number (or line number)				•		•	
Dates of record creation and filing (if shown)	•				•		

1. Or abstractor, editor, transcriber, or translator. The precise function of the individual should be noted.
2. Citations for film and electronic data cover: (*a*) details for the publication; and (*b*) details for the material reproduced within.

FIGURE 9. BASIC RULES *for* ARRANGING THE ELEMENTS

Bibliographic entries:

Two sequences are common.

- *Emphasis on location:* start citation with place; cite items in descending level of importance, ending with specific record or record group. Examples: see citation formats for baptismal record, deed, and marriage record (civil).

- *Emphasis on person:* start citation with person's surname then given name, followed by details of record. Examples: see citation formats for interview and letter.

As a rule,

- *Emphasis on location* is chosen if a number of records were used from that collection of records.

- *Emphasis on person* is chosen if only one record on a single individual is cited to that source.

Full v. short citations:

- *At first reference* to a source, all relevant elements are cited. See Primary Citation column of the format table.

- *At subsequent references* to the same source, a short form may be used. See Subsequent Citations column.

Shortened citations are used *only* for subsequent citations to a source that is already given in full.

Published v. unpublished volumes:

- *Published* volumes, microforms, CDs, and software use italics (or underscoring) in titles. In note format, their page numbers are preceded by a comma.

- *Unpublished* manuscripts, dissertations, and theses use quotation marks around titles. In note format, their page numbers are preceded by a comma.

- *Serial manuscript volumes* (courthouse books, church registers, etc.) use neither italics nor quotation marks. Titles are rendered precisely, with standard capitalization (i.e., all major words are capitalized; coordinating conjunctions, prepositions, and articles are lowercased—except for articles used as first word of titles).

As with essays in published serials, the page number is preceded by a colon.

Sequence of citation elements—unpublished documents:

- *Bibliographic entries* generally start with the broadest element and move to the most specific.

- *Note entries* generally start with the most specific element and move to the broadest.

Primary Citation (Endnotes or Footnotes)	Subsequent Citations (Endnotes or Footnotes)	Bibliographic Entry
ANCESTRAL FILE™ 1. E. Kay Kirkham, compiler, "William Dendy–Clary family group sheet" (undocumented); ancestral file numbers B4GH-JV and B4GH-K2, *Ancestral File*, version 4.13 (1994), Family History Library [FHL], Salt Lake City, Utah.	**ANCESTRAL FILE™** 1. Kirkham, "William Dendy–Clary Cargill family group sheet," FHL. *Ancestral File*.	**ANCESTRAL FILE™** *Ancestral File*, version 4.13. Family History Library, Salt Lake City, 1994.
ARTICLE (JOURNAL) 1. Louise F. Johnson, "Testing Popular Lore: Marmaduke Swearingen a.k.a. Chief Blue Jacket," *National Genealogical Society Quarterly* 82 (September 1994): 165–78.[1]	**ARTICLE (JOURNAL)** 1. Johnson, "Testing Popular Lore: Marmaduke Swearingen a.k.a. Chief Blue Jacket," 165–78.	**ARTICLE (JOURNAL)** Johnson, Louise F. "Testing Popular Lore: Marmaduke Swearingen a.k.a. Chief Blue Jacket." *National Genealogical Society Quarterly* 82 (September 1994).
ARTICLE (SERIALIZED; ANNOTATED CITATION) 1. John Frederick Dorman, "[*Name of*] County, Virginia, 1800 Tax List," *The Virginia Genealogist*, ongoing series from volume 3 (January/March 1959) to present. The series begins with Albemarle County.[2]	**ARTICLE (SERIALIZED; ANNOTATED CITATION)** 1. Dorman, "[*Name of*] County, Virginia, 1800 Tax List," *Virginia Genealogist*, ongoing series from volume 3 (January/March 1959) to present.	**ARTICLE (SERIALIZED; ANNOTATED CITATION)** Dorman, John Frederick. "[*Name of*] County, Virginia, 1800 Tax List." *The Virginia Genealogist*. Ongoing series from volume 3, January/March 1959.

1. Citations to periodicals should include the month/season in which an issue was published or the issue number. Many local and family periodicals begin renumbering each issue with page 1, causing several issues per year to contain the same pagination. This manual recommends month/season rather than issue number, because typographic errors occur more often with numbers than words. If your text refers to material that appears only in part of the article, the citation should be to the specific part.

2. A generic citation of this type is acceptable only if the entire series is being referenced. To support a statement from one particular part of this series, we should use the basic article form in the Louise F. Johnson example above.

Primary Citation (Endnotes or Footnotes)	Subsequent Citations (Endnotes or Footnotes)	Bibliographic Entry
BAPTISMAL RECORD 1. Book 7, Baptisms of Slaves, 1826-31: entry 31 (1830), unpaginated, Saint François Catholic Church, Natchitoches, Louisiana.	**BAPTISMAL RECORD** 1. Book 7, Baptisms of Slaves, 1826-31: entry 31 (1830), Saint François Church.	**BAPTISMAL RECORD** Louisiana. Natchitoches. Saint François Church. Baptisms of Slaves, 1826-31.
BIBLE RECORD (WITH PROVENANCE) 1. Family data, Charles Bertrand Family Bible, *La Sainte Bible*, new edition (Paris: Pourrat Frères, 1838); original owned in 1996 by Gary B. Mills (1732 Ridgedale Drive; Tuscaloosa, AL 35406). The Bertrand Family Bible passed from Charles to his daughter Henriette (Bertrand) Charleville, to her daughter Minerva (Charleville) Mills, to her grandson, Gary B. Mills.	**BIBLE RECORD (WITH PROVENANCE)** 1. Charles Bertrand Family Bible.	**BIBLE RECORD (WITH PROVENANCE)** Bertrand, Charles, family data. In *La Sainte Bible*. New edition. Paris: Pourrat Frères, 1838. Original owned in 1996 by Gary B. Mills, 1732 Ridgedale Drive; Tuscaloosa, AL 35406-1942.
BIRTH REGISTRATION (LOCAL LEVEL) 1. Alma Roeseke, birth certificate no. 1753 (1886), Clerk's Office, City Hall, Chicago, Illinois. *or* 1. Rosa B. Miller entry, Eaton County Births, Liber 1: 118, no. 1743, County Clerk's Office, Charlotte, Michigan.	**BIRTH REGISTRATION (LOCAL LEVEL)** 1. Alma Roeseke, Chicago birth certificate no. 1753 (1886). *or* 1. Rosa B. Miller entry, Eaton County Births, Liber 1: 118, no. 1743.	**BIRTH REGISTRATION (LOCAL LEVEL)** Illinois. Chicago. Clerk's Office, City Hall. Birth Registrations. Alma Roeseke entry. *or* Michigan. Eaton County. County Clerk's Office, Charlotte. Birth Registers. Rosa B. Miller entry.

Primary Citation (Endnotes or Footnotes)	Subsequent Citations (Endnotes or Footnotes)	Bibliographic Entry
BIRTH REGISTRATION (STATE LEVEL) 1. Philip Daniel Mills, birth certificate [long form] no. 134-85-001195 (1985), North Carolina Division of Health Services–Vital Records Branch, Raleigh.[3]	**BIRTH REGISTRATION (STATE LEVEL)** 1. Philip Daniel Mills, North Carolina birth certificate, no. 134-85-001195 (1985).	**BIRTH REGISTRATION (STATE LEVEL)** North Carolina. Raleigh. Division of Health Services–Vital Records Branch. Philip Daniel Mills birth certificate.
BOOK (AUTHORED) 1. Daniel F. Littlefield Jr., *Africans and Creeks from the Colonial Period to the Civil War* (Westport, Connecticut: Greenwood Press, 1979), 79–80.[4]	**BOOK (AUTHORED)** 1. Littlefield, *Africans and Creeks*, 79–80.	**BOOK (AUTHORED)** Littlefield, Daniel F. Jr. *Africans and Creeks from the Colonial Period to the Civil War.* Westport, Connecticut: Greenwood Press, 1979.
BOOK (AUTHORED BY AN AGENCY) 1. Bureau of the Census, *Heads of Families at the First Census of the United States Taken in the Year 1790: Connecticut* (Washington: Government Printing Office, 1908), 53.[4]	**BOOK (AUTHORED BY AN AGENCY)** 1. Bureau of the Census, *Heads of Families . . . 1790: Connecticut*, 53.[5]	**BOOK (AUTHORED BY AN AGENCY)** Bureau of the Census. *Heads of Families at the First Census of the United States Taken in the Year 1790: Connecticut.* Washington: Government Printing Office, 1908.

3. Regarding the inclusion of the year of registration: in North Carolina and various other states, the year appears in the registration number (middle set of digits).

4. If a city name is well known, as with Washington above, it is not necessary to give the state of location. If the city name is not well known, as with Westport, Connecticut, its state should be identified—unless another part of the publication data makes the state self-evident (example: Baton Rouge: Louisiana State University Press). If two cities are cited (example: New York and London), it is not necessary to cite both. Logically, Americans would cite the New York office; Britishers would cite the London office.

5. Ellipsis points are commonly used if a middle or ending portion of the title is deleted. It is best to retain the first part of a title, except when the first word is *A, An,* or *The.*

Primary Citation (Endnotes or Footnotes)	*Subsequent Citations* (Endnotes or Footnotes)	*Bibliographic Entry*
BOOK (AUTHOR UNIDENTIFIED BUT KNOWN) 1. [Meredith B. Colket Jr. and Frank E. Bridgers], *Guide to Genealogical Records in the National Archives* (Washington: National Archives and Records Service, 1964), 116.[6]	**BOOK (AUTHOR UNIDENTIFIED BUT KNOWN)** 1. [Colket and Bridgers], *Guide to Genealogical Records in the National Archives*, 116.	**BOOK (AUTHOR UNIDENTIFIED BUT KNOWN)** [Colket, Meredith B., Jr., and Frank E. Bridgers]. *Guide to Genealogical Records in the National Archives.* Washington: National Archives and Records Service, 1964.
BOOK (AUTHOR UNKNOWN) 1. [Anonymous], *Guide to Genealogical Research in the National Archives* (Washington: National Archives and Records Service, 1982), 116.	**BOOK (AUTHOR UNKNOWN)** 1. *Guide to Genealogical Research in the National Archives*, 116.	**BOOK (AUTHOR UNKNOWN)** *Guide to Genealogical Research in the National Archives.* Washington: National Archives and Records Service, 1982.
BOOK (COMPILED RECORDS) 1. Carol Wells, compiler, *Natchez Postscripts, 1781–1798* (Bowie, Maryland: Heritage Books, 1992), 66.	**BOOK (COMPILED RECORDS)** 1. Wells, *Natchez Postscripts, 1781–1798*, 66.	**BOOK (COMPILED RECORDS)** Wells, Carol, compiler. *Natchez Postscripts, 1781–1798.* Bowie, Maryland: Heritage Books, 1992.
BOOK (EDITED) 1. John H. Peterson Jr., editor, *A Choctaw Source Book* (New York: Garland Publishing, 1985), xi.	**BOOK (EDITED)** 1. Peterson, *Choctaw Source Book*, xi.	**BOOK (EDITED)** Peterson, John H., Jr., editor. *A Choctaw Source Book.* New York: Garland Publishing, 1985.

6. Many writers and editors dispense with the appellation *Anonymous* and begin the citation with the title of the book or article.

Primary Citation (Endnotes or Footnotes)	Subsequent Citations (Endnotes or Footnotes)	Bibliographic Entry
BOOK (MULTI-AUTHORED) 1. Loretto Dennis Szucs and Sandra Hargreaves Luebking, *The Archives: A Guide to the National Archives Field Branches* (Salt Lake City: Ancestry Publishing, 1988), 6.	**BOOK (MULTI-AUTHORED)** 1. Szucs and Luebking, *The Archives*, 6.	**BOOK (MULTI-AUTHORED)** Szucs, Loretto Dennis, and Sandra Hargreaves Luebking. *The Archives: A Guide to the National Archives Field Branches.* Salt Lake City: Ancestry Publishing, 1988.
BOOK (MULTI-VOLUME) 1. Robert Charles Anderson, *The Great Migration Begins: Immigrants to New England, 1620–1633,* 3 volumes (Boston: New England Historic Genealogical Society, 1995), 1: 22.	**BOOK (MULTI-VOLUME)** 1. Anderson, *The Great Migration Begins,* 1: 22.	**BOOK (MULTI-VOLUME)** Anderson, Robert Charles. *The Great Migration Begins: Immigrants to New England, 1620–1633.* 3 volumes. Boston: New England Historic Genealogical Society, 1995.
BOOK (MULTI-VOLUME, COMPENDIUM) (COMPOSED OF EARLIER JOURNAL ESSAYS) 1. Landon C. Bell, "Field Jefferson's Second Wife," *Genealogies of Virginia Families from Tyler's Quarterly Historical and Genealogical Magazine,* 4 volumes (Baltimore: Genealogical Publishing Company, 1981), 2: ix, 457–64; originally published in *Tyler's Quarterly* 13 (July 1931): 15–23.	**BOOK (MULTI-VOLUME, COMPENDIUM) (COMPOSED OF EARLIER JOURNAL ESSAYS)** 1. Bell, "Field Jefferson's Second Wife," *Genealogies of Virginia Families,* 2: ix, 457–64.	**BOOK (MULTI-VOLUME, COMPENDIUM) (COMPOSED OF EARLIER JOURNAL ESSAYS)** Bell, Landon C. "Field Jefferson's Second Wife," *Genealogies of Virginia Families from Tyler's Quarterly Historical and Genealogical Magazine,* 4 volumes. Baltimore: Genealogical Publishing Company, 1981. Originally published in *Tyler's Quarterly* 13 (July 1931): 15–23.

Primary Citation (Endnotes or Footnotes)	*Subsequent Citations* (Endnotes or Footnotes)	*Bibliographic Entry*
BOOK (ONE OF A SERIES) 1. GeLee Corley Hendrix, *Research in South Carolina*, National Genealogical Society Research in the States Series (Arlington, Virginia: NGS, 1992), 13.	**BOOK (ONE OF A SERIES)** 1. Hendrix, *Research in South Carolina*, 13.	**BOOK (ONE OF A SERIES)** Hendrix, GeLee Corley. *Research in South Carolina*. National Genealogical Society Research in the States Series. Arlington, Virginia: NGS, 1992.
BOOK (PAGINATED, WITH NUMBERED ENTRIES) 1. Margaret M. Hofmann, compiler, *Genealogical Abstracts of Wills, 1758–1824; Halifax County, North Carolina* (Weldon, North Carolina: Roanoke News Company, 1970), 182, no. 1017.	**BOOK (PAGINATED, WITH NUMBERED ENTRIES)** 1. Hofmann, *Genealogical Abstracts of Wills, 1758–1824; Halifax County, North Carolina*, 182, no. 1017.	**BOOK (PAGINATED, WITH NUMBERED ENTRIES)** Hofmann, Margaret M., compiler. *Genealogical Abstracts of Wills, 1758–1824; Halifax County, North Carolina*. Weldon, North Carolina: Roanoke News Company, 1970.
BOOK (PAGINATION NOT GIVEN) 1. *St. James Catholic Church, Gadsden, Alabama, 1876–1976* (Gadsden: The parish, 1976), unpaginated, 10th page.	**BOOK (PAGINATION NOT GIVEN)** 1. *St. James Catholic Church, Gadsden*, unpaginated, 10th page.	**BOOK (PAGINATION NOT GIVEN)** *St. James Catholic Church, Gadsden, Alabama, 1876–1976*. Gadsden: The parish, 1976.
BOOK (PRIVATELY PRINTED) 1. John A. Brayton, *The Five Thomas Harrises of Isle of Wight County, Virginia* (Winston-Salem, North Carolina: Privately printed, 1995), 99.	**BOOK (PRIVATELY PRINTED)** 1. Brayton, *Five Thomas Harrises*, 99.	**BOOK (PRIVATELY PRINTED)** Brayton, John A. *The Five Thomas Harrises of Isle of Wight County, Virginia*. Winston-Salem, North Carolina: Privately printed, 1995.

Primary Citation (Endnotes or Footnotes)	Subsequent Citations (Endnotes or Footnotes)	Bibliographic Entry
BOOK (PUBLICATION DATE NOT GIVEN)[7] 1. Bob Blankenship, *Cherokee Roots* (Gatlinburg, Tennessee: Buckhorn Press, no date), 7.	**BOOK (PUBLICATION DATE NOT GIVEN)** 1. Blankenship, *Cherokee Roots*, 7.	**BOOK (PUBLICATION DATE NOT GIVEN)** Blankenship, Bob. *Cherokee Roots*. Gatlinburg, Tennessee: Buckhorn Press, no date.
BOOK (PUBLICATION PLACE NOT GIVEN) 1. Juanita Gerling, *The Poly Family History* (No place: privately printed, 1989), 9.	**BOOK (PUBLICATION PLACE NOT GIVEN)** 1. Gerling, *Poly Family History*, 9.	**BOOK (PUBLICATION PLACE NOT GIVEN)** Gerling, Juanita. *The Poly Family History*. No place: privately printed, 1989.
BOOK (PUBLISHER NOT GIVEN) 1. *Official Commemorative Book for the Sesquicentennial of Louisville, Ohio* (Louisville: no publisher, 1984), 10.	**BOOK (PUBLISHER NOT GIVEN)** 1. *Official Commemorative Book . . . of Louisville, Ohio*, 10.	**BOOK (PUBLISHER NOT GIVEN)** *Official Commemorative Book for the Sesquicentennial of Louisville, Ohio*. Louisville: no publisher, 1984.
BOOK (REPRINT) 1. Oscar Kuhns, *The German and Swiss Settlements of Colonial Pennsylvania* (1901; reprint, Bowie, Maryland: Heritage Books, 1989), 15.[8]	**BOOK (REPRINT)** 1. Kuhns, *German and Swiss Settlements of Colonial Pennsylvania*, 15.	**BOOK (REPRINT)** Kuhns, Oscar. *The German and Swiss Settlements of Colonial Pennsylvania*. 1901. Reprint, Bowie, Maryland: Heritage Books, 1989.

7. When publication data cannot be found on the title page, it might be obtainable from the copyright notice, from a dated preface, or from library cataloging information.

8. It is important to include the original publication date. Whether a book is a modern compilation or whether it was researched and written fifty, a hundred, or more years ago will often make a difference in the analysis of its data.

Primary Citation (Endnotes or Footnotes)	Subsequent Citations (Endnotes or Footnotes)	Bibliographic Entry
BOOK (REVISED EDITION) 1. Val D. Greenwood, *The Researcher's Guide to American Genealogy*, 2d edition (Baltimore: Genealogical Publishing Company, 1990), 321–43.	**BOOK (REVISED EDITION)** 1. Greenwood, *Researcher's Guide to American Genealogy*, 321–43.	**BOOK (REVISED EDITION)** Greenwood, Val D. *The Researcher's Guide to American Genealogy*. 2d edition. Baltimore: Genealogical Publishing Company, 1990.
BOOK CHAPTER 1. William Thorndale, "Land and Tax Records," in *The Source: A Guidebook of American Genealogy*, Arlene Eakle and Johni Cerny, editors (Salt Lake City: Ancestry Publishing, 1984), 216–53.	**BOOK CHAPTER** 1. Thorndale, "Land and Tax Records," 216–53.	**BOOK CHAPTER** Thorndale, William. "Land and Tax Records." In *The Source: A Guidebook of American Genealogy*. Arlene Eakle and Johni Cerny, editors. Salt Lake City: Ancestry Publishing, 1984.
BOUNTY-LAND FILE (FEDERAL, UNFILMED) 1. Jacob Ambriester bounty-land application (private, 2d Pennsylvania Volunteers), warrant no. 50768; Case Files of Bounty-Land Applications Based on Service between 1812 and 1855; Pension and Bounty-Land Warrant Application Files, 1800–1960; Records of the Veterans Administration, Record Group 15; National Archives, Washington.⁹	**BOUNTY-LAND FILE (FEDERAL, UNFILMED)** 1. Jacob Ambriester bounty-land application. warrant no. 50768, Veterans Administration, National Archives.	**BOUNTY-LAND FILE (FEDERAL, UNFILMED)** United States. National Archives, Washington, D.C. Records of the Veterans Administration, Record Group 15. Case Files of Bounty-Land Applications Based on Service between 1812 and 1855; Pension and Bounty-Land Warrant Application Files, 1800–1960.

9. This National Archives citation is considerably lengthier than those genealogists commonly use. It follows NA's requested form.

Primary Citation (Endnotes or Footnotes)	Subsequent Citations (Endnotes or Footnotes)	Bibliographic Entry
CD-ROM (PRODUCED FROM ORIGINAL RECORDS) 1. United States, General Land Office, *Automated Records Project; Pre-1908 Homestead & Cash Entry Patents: Arkansas*, CD-ROM (Springfield, Virginia: Bureau of Land Management, Eastern States, 1994), Richard Stiles entry, SW¼, section 30, township 6N, range 14W.[10]	**CD-ROM** (PRODUCED FROM ORIGINAL RECORDS) 1. Richard Stiles entry, SW¼, section 30, township 6N, range 14W, *Automated Records Project; Pre-1908 . . . Patents: Arkansas.*	**CD-ROM** (PRODUCED FROM ORIGINAL RECORDS) United States. General Land Office. *Automated Records Project; Pre-1908 Homestead & Cash Entry Patents: Arkansas.* CD-ROM. Springfield, Virginia: Bureau of Land Management, Eastern States, 1994.
CD-ROM (PRODUCED FROM PRIOR PUBLICATION) 1. Nicholas Shown entry, FamilyFinder database, *Family Tree Maker,* CD-ROM (Fremont, California: Banner Blue Software, 1994), citing *Archive CD-153* (Orem, Utah: Automated Archives, no date). This data set is based on the census-index series compiled by Ronald V. Jackson et al. (Salt Lake City [and elsewhere]: Accelerated Indexing Systems, 1970s–1980s).	**CD-ROM** (PRODUCED FROM PRIOR PUBLICATION) 1. Nicholas Shown entry, FamilyFinder database, *Family Tree Maker.*	**CD-ROM** (PRODUCED FROM PRIOR PUBLICATION) FamilyFinder database. *Family Tree Maker,* CD-ROM. Fremont, California: Banner Blue Software, 1994.

10. More than one Richard Stiles entry exists in this database. Hence, it is necessary to identify the specific entry of relevance. Regarding the publisher: the agency's full identification is Department of the Interior; Bureau of Land Management, Eastern States. In such cases involving a bureau within an agency (including Bureau of the Census and Bureau of Indian Affairs), most style manuals permit citing only the bureau and not the department that oversees it.

Primary Citation (Endnotes or Footnotes)	Subsequent Citations (Endnotes or Footnotes)	Bibliographic Entry
CEMETERY MARKER (PUBLISHED) 1. Elizabeth Doherty Herzfeld, *Old Cemetery Burials of Milwaukee County, Wisconsin* (Bowie, Maryland: Heritage Books, 1995), 95 (Greenwood Cemetery).	**CEMETERY MARKER (PUBLISHED)** 1. Herzfeld, *Old Cemetery Burials of Milwaukee County, Wisconsin*, 95.	**CEMETERY MARKER (PUBLISHED)** Herzfeld, Elizabeth Doherty. *Old Cemetery Burials of Milwaukee County, Wisconsin.* Bowie, Maryland: Heritage Books, 1995.
CEMETERY MARKER (RURAL, SMALL) 1. Samuel Witter tombstone, Brian Cemetery, Lawrence County, Illinois (5.5 miles SW of Sumner in section 30, township 3N, range 13W); photographed by Eugene Laws, landowner, February 1974.	**CEMETERY MARKER (RURAL, SMALL)** 1. Samuel Witter tombstone, Brian Cemetery, Lawrence County, Illinois.	**CEMETERY MARKER (RURAL, SMALL)** Illinois. Lawrence County. Brian Cemetery. Tombstone data.
CEMETERY MARKER (URBAN, LARGE) 1. Eggbert Petersen tombstone, section 555C, Waldheim Cemetery, Forest Park (Cook County), Illinois; transcribed by the writer on 10 July 1988.	**CEMETERY MARKER (URBAN, LARGE)** 1. Eggbert Petersen tombstone, Waldheim Cemetery, Forest Park, Illinois.	**CEMETERY MARKER (URBAN, LARGE)** Illinois. Cook County. Waldheim Cemetery, Forest Park. Tombstone data.
CENSUS, FEDERAL, 1790–1840 (FILMED) 1. G. W. Frame household. 1840 U.S. census, Claiborne Parish, Louisiana, page 94, line 2; National Archives micropublication M704, roll 127.	**CENSUS, FEDERAL, 1790–1840 (FILMED)** 1. 1840 U.S. cens., Claiborne Par., La., p. 94, line 2.[11]	**CENSUS, FEDERAL, 1790–1840 (FILMED)** Louisiana. Claiborne Parish. U.S. census, 1840. Micropublication M704, roll 127. Washington: National Archives.

11. Many genealogists liberally abbreviate their references to censuses (including state name and county designation) because they cite this resource so extensively. It is best to spell out all words in the first citation to a particular census, particularly for post-1840 returns that contain many elements whose abbreviations may not be recognized by beginning researchers.

Primary Citation (Endnotes or Footnotes)	Subsequent Citations (Endnotes or Footnotes)	Bibliographic Entry
CENSUS, FEDERAL, 1850–70 (FILMED) 1. Abner Lake household, 1870 U.S. census, Lawrence County, Illinois, population schedule, Christy township, Bridgeport post office, page 29, dwelling 38, family 38; National Archives micropublication M593, roll 245.	**CENSUS, FEDERAL, 1850–70 (FILMED)** 1. 1870 U.S. census, Lawrence County, Illinois, population schedule, Christy township, page 29, dwelling 38, family 38. [*Or abbreviate as per page 73, column 2, last entry.*]	**CENSUS, FEDERAL, 1850–70 (FILMED)** Illinois. Lawrence County. 1870 U.S. census, population schedule. Micropublication M593, roll 245. Washington: National Archives.
CENSUS, FEDERAL, 1880–1920 (FILMED) 1. Mortimer Edwards household, 1880 U.S. census, Winona County, Minnesota, population schedule, town of Winona, enumeration district [ED] 289, supervisor's district [SD] 1, sheet 19, dwelling 172, family 182; National Archives micropublication T9, roll 637.[12]	**CENSUS, FEDERAL, 1880–1920 (FILMED)** 1. 1880 U.S. census, Winona County, Minnesota, population schedule, Winona, ED 289, SD 1, sheet 19, dwelling 172, family 182. [*Or abbreviate as per page 73, column 2, last entry.*]	**CENSUS, FEDERAL, 1880–1920 (FILMED)** Minnesota. Winona County. 1880 U.S. census, population schedule. Micropublication T9, roll 637. Washington: National Archives.

12.   The 1880 entry used here identifies the household by dwelling and family numbers can be cited, line numbers should be. Where dwelling and family numbers exist, it is better to use them in preference to line numbers, because the dwelling and family numbers reveal clues to family groupings.

Some censuses also carry stamped page numbers as well as sheet numbers. If both are present, it is wise to record both. In either case, a researcher should take care to note whether the sheet/page numbers represent the entire census, the supervisor's district, the enumerator's district, or just a ward or other political subdivision. The ability to relocate a particular entry at a later date, especially in large urban areas, can depend upon the care taken in recording the page number.

Primary Citation (Endnotes or Footnotes)	*Subsequent Citations* (Endnotes or Footnotes)	*Bibliographic Entry*
CENSUS, FEDERAL (LOCAL/STATE COPY) 1. Charles C. Sammonds household, 1860 U.S. census, Pike County, Alabama, population schedule, Pea River post office, page 324, dwelling 1034, family 1046; county-level copy, Probate Judge's Office, Pike County Courthouse, Troy, Alabama.[13]	**CENSUS, FEDERAL (LOCAL/STATE COPY)** 1. 1860 U.S. census, Pike County, Alabama, population schedule, Pea River post office, page 324, dwelling 1034, family 1046; county-level copy. [*Or abbreviate as per page 73, column 2, last entry.*]	**CENSUS, FEDERAL (LOCAL/STATE COPY)** Alabama. Pike County. 1860 U.S. census, population schedule. County-level copy. Probate Judge's Office, Troy, Alabama.
CENSUS, STATE 1. Robert Morton household, 1895 Kansas state census, Jackson County, population schedule, Whiting township, page 2519, line 25; microcopy K63, Kansas State Historical Society, Topeka.	**CENSUS, STATE** 1. 1895 Kansas state census, Jackson County, population schedule, Whiting township, page 2519, line 25. [*Or abbreviate as per page 73, column 2, last entry.*]	**CENSUS, STATE** Kansas. Jackson County. 1895 state census, population schedule. Kansas State Historical Society, Topeka.
CENSUS COMPENDIUM 1. Census Office, *Statistics of the United States (Including Mortality, Property, &c.) in 1860* (Washington: Government Printing Office, 1866), lxi-lxii, "Table OO, Nativity of Americans Residing in Each State and Territory."	**CENSUS COMPENDIUM** 1. *Statistics of the United States . . . in 1860,* lxi-lxii.	**CENSUS COMPENDIUM** Census Office. *Statistics of the United States (Including Mortality, Property, &c.) in 1860* (Washington: Government Printing Office, 1866).

13. When using a local or state copy of the federal census, rather than NA's microfilmed copy, the researcher should say so. Local and state copies, when and where created and extant, often contain significant differences in comparison to the copies submitted to federal authorities. The example cited above is one such case.

Primary Citation (Endnotes or Footnotes)	Subsequent Citations (Endnotes or Footnotes)	Bibliographic Entry
CHURCH MINUTE 1. Cezar Kenedy, colored, ordained as preacher, 1st Sunday in October 1821, Flint River Baptist Association Minutes, 1814–21, Madison County, Alabama; microcopy SCB 185, Samford University Archives, Birmingham, Alabama. **CHURCH RECORD** See BAPTISMAL RECORD *and* MARRIAGE RECORD.	**CHURCH MINUTE** 1. Kenedy ordination, Minute Book 1: 66–67, Flint River Baptist Association.	**CHURCH MINUTE** Alabama. Madison County. Flint River Baptist Association. Minutes, 1814–21. Microcopy SCB 185, Samford University Archives, Birmingham, Alabama.
CITY (OR COUNTY) DIRECTORY 1. *Cohen's New Orleans Directory, Including Jefferson City, Carrollton, Gretna, Algiers, and McDonough, for 1854; . . . Portraits of the Citizens of New Orleans, with Their Biographies; Also, A Tableau of the Yellow Fever [Deaths] of 1853* (New Orleans: The Picayune, 1854), 19.[14]	**CITY (OR COUNTY) DIRECTORY** 1. *Cohen's New Orleans [Area] Directory,* 1854, 19.	**CITY (OR COUNTY) DIRECTORY** *Cohen's New Orleans Directory, Including Jefferson City, Carrollton, Gretna, Algiers, and McDonough, for 1854; . . . Portraits of the Citizens of New Orleans, with Their Biographies; Also, A Tableau of the Yellow Fever [Deaths] of 1853.* New Orleans: The Picayune, 1854.
COMPUTER SOFTWARE 1. *Roots V,* PC Software (Windsor, California: Commsoft, 1996), online "Help."	**COMPUTER SOFTWARE** 1. *Roots V,* online "Help."	**COMPUTER SOFTWARE** *Roots V,* PC Software. Windsor, California: Commsoft, 1996.

14. City and county directories often have exceedingly long subtitles, which practicality suggests should be shortened. In doing so, it is wise to retain in the title any references to special items that have significant genealogical value.

Primary Citation *(Endnotes or Footnotes)*	*Subsequent Citations* *(Endnotes or Footnotes)*	*Bibliographic Entry*
DAR GENEALOGICAL RECORDS COMMITTEE REPORT (LOCAL OR STATE COPY)[15] 1. Clara G. Mark, "Three Old Cemeteries along Zane's Trace in Salt Creek Township, Pickaway County, Ohio; Tarlton Cemetery, Stumpf or Jerusalem Cemetery, Imler Cemetery" (typescript, 1952–56, by Washington Court House [Ohio] Society, Daughters of the American Revolution), 16; copy at Ohio State Library, Columbus.	**DAR GENEALOGICAL RECORDS COMMITTEE REPORT (LOCAL OR STATE COPY)** 1. Mark, "Three Old Cemeteries along Zane's Trace." 16.	**DAR GENEALOGICAL RECORDS COMMITTEE REPORT (LOCAL OR STATE COPY)** Mark, Clara G. "Three Old Cemeteries along Zane's Trace in Salt Creek Township, Pickaway County, Ohio; Tarlton Cemetery, Stumpf or Jerusalem Cemetery, Imler Cemetery." Typescript, 1952–56, Washington Court House [Ohio] Society, Daughters of the American Revolution. Copy at Ohio State Library, Columbus.
DAR GENEALOGICAL RECORDS COMMITTEE REPORT—DAR LIBRARY COPY[15] 1. *Early Vital Records of Ohio: Three Old Cemeteries along Zane's Trace in Salt Creek Township, Pickaway County, Ohio; Tarlton Cemetery; Stumpf or Jerusalem Cemetery; Imler Cemetery* in *Ohio Daughters of the American Revolution [DAR], Genealogical Records Committee Report: Miscellaneous Records*, Series 1 (typescript serial, 1952–56; DAR Library, Washington), 16. These inscriptions were compiled by Clara G. Mark.	**DAR GENEALOGICAL RECORDS COMMITTEE REPORT—DAR LIBRARY COPY** 1. *Early Vital Records of Ohio: Three Old Cemeteries along Zane's Trace*, 16.	**DAR GENEALOGICAL RECORDS COMMITTEE REPORT—DAR LIBRARY COPY** *Early Vital Records of Ohio: Three Old Cemeteries along Zane's Trace in Salt Creek Township, Pickaway County, Ohio; Tarlton Cemetery; Stumpf or Jerusalem Cemetery; Imler Cemetery. Ohio Daughters of the American Revolution [DAR], Genealogical Records Committee Report: Miscellaneous Records*, Series 1. 1952–56; DAR Library, Washington.

15. Titles affixed to locally held compilations of this committee may differ from those assigned by the DAR Library, Washington. Also, local copies of these compilations are generally cited as typescripts—using quotation marks and citing a repository as well as the sponsoring society—because they have not been published. The DAR Library, which is attempting to provide overall organization to the national set, treats each as a serial—using italicized titles, serial numbers, and (when project is completed) volume numbers.

Primary Citation (Endnotes or Footnotes)	Subsequent Citations (Endnotes or Footnotes)	Bibliographic Entry
DAUGHTERS OF THE AMERICAN REVOLUTION [DAR] See also **LINEAGE APPLICATION.**		
DEATH REGISTRATION (LOCAL LEVEL) 1. Frances B. Whitney entry, Eaton County Deaths, Liber 2: 418, no. 110, County Clerk's Office, Charlotte, Michigan.	**DEATH REGISTRATION (LOCAL LEVEL)** 1. Eaton County Deaths, Liber 2: 418.	**DEATH REGISTRATION (LOCAL LEVEL)** Michigan. Eaton County. County Clerk's Office, Charlotte. Death Registers. Frances B. Whitney entry.
DEATH REGISTRATION (STATE LEVEL) 1. Floyd Finley Shown, death certificate no. 59-0024 (1959), Tennessee Department of Public Health, Nashville.	**DEATH REGISTRATION (STATE LEVEL)** 1. Floyd Finley Shown, Tennessee state death certificate 59-0024.	**DEATH REGISTRATION (STATE LEVEL)** Tennessee. Nashville. Department of Public Health. Death Registrations. Floyd Finley Shown certificate.
DEED (STATE LEVEL) 1. Secretary of State Deeds 30: 387–90, New York State Archives, Albany.	**DEED (STATE LEVEL)** 1. Secretary of State Deeds 30: 387–90, New York State Archives.	**DEED (STATE LEVEL)** New York. State Archives, Albany. Secretary of State Deeds, 1649–1846.
DEED (TOWN OR COUNTY LEVEL) 1. Providence Land Evidences, Book 4: 263, City Hall–Division of Archives and History, Providence, Rhode Island.[16]	**DEED (TOWN OR COUNTY LEVEL)** 1. Providence Land Evidences, 4: 263.	**DEED (TOWN OR COUNTY LEVEL)** Rhode Island. Providence. City Hall–Division of Archives and History. Land Evidences, 1721.

16. The identification of a deed's grantor and grantee and the nature of the document are optional in a citation. If these details are given in the text, there is no need to repeat them in the note.

Primary Citation (Endnotes or Footnotes)	*Subsequent Citations* (Endnotes or Footnotes)	*Bibliographic Entry*
DIARY OR JOURNAL (MANUSCRIPT) 1. "Journal of Sarah Jane (Hickman) Brown," (MS, 1896–1902; Fernwood Station, Mississippi; owned 1996 by her great-granddaughter, Anne S. Anderson; Post Office Box 1647; Gulfport, MS 39501.	**DIARY OR JOURNAL (MANUSCRIPT)** 1. "Journal of Sarah Jane (Hickman) Brown," 90.	**DIARY OR JOURNAL (MANUSCRIPT)** Brown, Sarah Jane (Hickman). "Journal." 1896–1902; Fernwood Station, Mississippi. Owned 1996 by great-granddaughter, Anne S. Anderson; Post Office Box 1647; Gulfport, MS 39501.
DIARY OR JOURNAL (PUBLISHED, EDITED) 1. W. P. Strickland, editor, *Autobiography of Peter Cartwright, the Backwoods Preacher* (Cincinnati: L. Swormstedt and A. Poe, 1856), 10.	**DIARY OR JOURNAL (PUBLISHED, EDITED)** 1. Strickland, *Autobiography of Peter Cartwright,* 10.	**DIARY OR JOURNAL (PUBLISHED, EDITED)** Strickland, W. P., editor. *Autobiography of Peter Cartwright, the Backwoods Preacher.* Cincinnati: L. Swormstedt and A. Poe, 1856.
DISSERTATION 1. Julie Winch, "The Leaders of Philadelphia's Black Community, 1789–1848" (Ph.D. dissertation, Bryn Mawr College, 1982), 23.	**DISSERTATION** 1. Winch, "Leaders of Philadelphia's Black Community," 23.	**DISSERTATION** Winch, Julie. "The Leaders of Philadelphia's Black Community, 1789–1848." Ph.D. dissertation, Bryn Mawr College, 1982.
DISSERTATION (MICROFILMED) 1. Gary B. Mills, "The Forgotten People: Cane River's Creoles of Color" (Ph.D. dissertation, Mississippi State University, 1974), microfilm edition (Ann Arbor, Michigan: University Microfilms, 1974), 323.	**DISSERTATION (MICROFILMED)** 1. Mills, "The Forgotten People," 323.	**DISSERTATION (MICROFILMED)** Mills, Gary B. "The Forgotten People: Cane River's Creoles of Color." Ph.D. dissertation, Mississippi State University, 1974. Microfilm edition. Ann Arbor, Michigan: University Microfilms, 1974.

Primary Citation (Endnotes or Footnotes)	Subsequent Citations (Endnotes or Footnotes)	Bibliographic Entry
E-MAIL MESSAGE 1. Christopher Nordmann, "Rochon Baptisms of Mobile: Translated Abstracts," e-mail message from <104274.1313@compuserve.com> (2767A Mary Avenue; St. Louis, MO 63144-2725) to author, 12 January 1997.[17]	**E-MAIL MESSAGE** 1. Nordmann, "Rochon Baptisms of Mobile: Translated Abstracts," e-mail to author, 12 January 1997.	**E-MAIL MESSAGE** Nordmann, Christopher. "Rochon Baptisms of Mobile: Translated Abstracts." E-mail message from <104274.1313@compuserve.com> at 2767A Mary Avenue; St. Louis, MO 63144-2725. 12 January 1997.
ELECTRONIC DATABASE (FAMILY FILE)[18] 1. Gowen Research Foundation, Electronic Library, online <http:\\www.llano.net/gowen>, Arlee Gowen, web master <gowen@llano.net> (5708 Gary Avenue; Lubbock, TX 79413), downloaded 15 November 1996, page 7.[19]	**ELECTRONIC DATABASE (FAMILY FILE)** 1. Gowen Research Foundation, Electronic Library, 15 November 1996, page 7.	**ELECTRONIC DATABASE (FAMILY FILE)** Gowen Research Foundation, Electronic Library. Online <http://www.llano.net/gowen>, Arlee Gowen, web master <gowen@llano.net> and 5708 Gary Avenue; Lubbock, TX 79413. Text downloaded 15 November 1996.

17. Because address changes in electronic mail and access ramps are far more frequent than changes of physical address, it is advisable to obtain postal addresses for originators of all electronically published genealogical material that is downloaded into personal files. Regarding the angle brackets: the less-than (<) and greater-than (>) symbols are a common way to mark the beginning and end of an electronic address; they are not part of the address itself.

18. Ideal citation styles for materials distributed online but not published in paper form are yet to be decided. This manual treats such material as manuscripts (i.e., unpublished), realizing that some readers will dissent. Genealogical standards expect that publications of significance should be available for future generations, and online transmission does not yet offer that kind of permanence—except as downloaded manuscripts, held thereafter in private files. A number of web sites offer helpful guidance on this issue of sound online citations. See the bibliography.

19. The date of downloading and/or printout should be noted, because many electronic documents undergo frequent revision.

Primary Citation (Endnotes or Footnotes)	*Subsequent Citations* (Endnotes or Footnotes)	*Bibliographic Entry*
ELECTRONIC FILE (**IMAGE FROM PRIVATE FILES—ANNOTATED**) 1. Floyd F. Shown and Mrs. Thelma [Thulmar] Carver, marriage certificate, 24 March 1931, Bolivar County, Mississippi. Image file "Shown12," scanned 15 November 1996 by Elizabeth Shown Mills <eshown@msn.com> (1732 Ridgedale Drive; Tuscaloosa, AL 35406), from original document in her possession. Image has been retouched by Mills to remove stains; she attests that no information has been altered. File provided to author by Mills in January 1997.	**ELECTRONIC FILE** (**IMAGE FROM PRIVATE FILES—ANNOTATED**) 1. Floyd F. Shown and Mrs. Thelma Carver, marriage certificate, image file "Shown12," Elizabeth Shown Mills to author.	**ELECTRONIC FILE** (**IMAGE FROM PRIVATE FILES—ANNOTATED**) Shown, Floyd F. and Mrs. Thelma [Thulmar] Carver, Marriage certificate, 24 March 1931, Bolivar County, Mississippi. Image file "Shown12," scanned 15 November 1996 by Elizabeth Shown Mills <eshown@msn.com> (1732 Ridgedale Drive; Tuscaloosa, AL 35406-1942). Original document owned in 1997 by Mills.
ELECTRONIC FILE (**IMAGE FROM PUBLIC ARCHIVES**) 1. Photo: Private Edmund Ruffin, by Matthew Brady; Pictures of the Civil War, Select Audiovisual Records; National Archives and Records Administration, Washington. Online <http://clio.nara.gov:70/I/inform/dc/audvis/still/civwar.html>; printout dated 29 March 1996.	**ELECTRONIC FILE** (**IMAGE FROM PUBLIC ARCHIVES**) 1. Private Edmund Ruffin photo, by Matthew Brady.	**ELECTRONIC FILE** (**IMAGE FROM PUBLIC ARCHIVES**) Ruffin, Edmund, Private. Photo by Matthew Brady. Pictures of the Civil War; Select Audiovisual Records; National Archives and Records Administration, Washington. Online <http://clio.nara.gov:70/I/inform/dc/audvis/still/civwar.html; file CIVIL159.JPG>. Printout dated 29 March 1996.

Primary Citation (Endnotes or Footnotes)	Subsequent Citations (Endnotes or Footnotes)	Bibliographic Entry
ELECTRONIC FILE—LISTSERVE MESSAGE 1. Daphne Gentry (Library of Virginia, Richmond), unidentified "report" quoted at length by Jon Kukla, in "Virginia Personal Property Tax Records as a Research Source," <Jon@HNOC.ORG>, listserve message to IEAHCNET list <IEAHCNET@H-NET.MSU.EDU>, 18 November 1996. Printout dated 22 November 1996.	**ELECTRONIC FILE—LISTSERVE MESSAGE** 1. Gentry, untitled report, in Kukla, "Virginia Personal Property Tax Records as a Research Source," listserve message, 18 November 1996.	**ELECTRONIC FILE—LISTSERVE MESSAGE** Gentry, Daphne. [Unidentified report.] In Jon Kukla, "Virginia Personal Property Tax Records as a Research Source." Listserve message from <Jon@HNOC.ORG> to IEAHCNET list <IEAHCNET@H-NET.MSU.EDU>. 18 November 1996.
ELECTRONIC WEB SITE 1. Index to Texas Confederate Pension Records, Archives Division, Texas State Library, online <http://link.tsl.state.tx.us/c/compt/index.html>, Minshew data downloaded 16 November 1996.	**ELECTRONIC WEB SITE** 1. Index to Texas Confederate Pension Records, online <http://link.tsl.state.tx.us/c/compt.html>.	**ELECTRONIC WEB SITE** Texas. Archives Division, Texas State Library, Austin. Confederate Pension Records, Index. Online <http://link.tsl.state.tx.us/c/compt/index.html>. Minshew data downloaded 16 November 1996.
ELECTRONICALLY PUBLISHED PAPER (PREVIOUSLY PUBLISHED IN HARD COPY) 1. "Records of District Courts of the United States (Record Group 21)," part 2, unpaginated, of *Black Studies: A Select Catalog of National Archives Microfilm Publications*, online <http://gopher.nara.gov:70/1/about/publ/micro/blkstd/>, printout dated 1 August 1996. Previously published in hard copy (Washington: National Archives Trust Fund Board, 1984).	**ELECTRONICALLY PUBLISHED PAPER (PREVIOUSLY PUBLISHED IN HARD COPY)** 1. *Black Studies . . . National Archives Microfilm Publications*, online, part 2, unpaginated.	**ELECTRONICALLY PUBLISHED PAPER (PREVIOUSLY PUBLISHED IN HARD COPY)** *Black Studies: A Select Catalog of National Archives Microfilm Publications.* Washington: National Archives Trust Fund Board, 1984. On-line <http://gopher.nara.gov:70/1/about/publ/micro/blkstd>. Printout dated 1 August 1996.

Primary Citation (Endnotes or Footnotes)	Subsequent Citations (Endnotes or Footnotes)	Bibliographic Entry
FAMILY GROUP SHEET (WITH ANNOTATION) 1. Jane Doe, "John Jones–Mary Smith family group sheet," supplied 23 November 1989 by Doe (111 Main Street; Anytown, US 00000). This sheet offers only a generic list of materials consulted.	**FAMILY GROUP SHEET (WITH ANNOTATION)** 1. Doe, "John Jones–Mary Smith family group sheet," inadequately documented.	**FAMILY GROUP SHEET (WITH ANNOTATION)** Doe, Jane. "John Jones–Mary Smith family group sheet." Compiled 23 November 1989. Available from compiler at 111 Main Street; Anytown; US 00000.
[FHL] FAMILY HISTORY LIBRARY[20] *See also* ANCESTRAL FILE, INTERNATIONAL GENEALOGICAL INDEX, *and* SOCIAL SECURITY DEATH INDEX.		
FHL MICROCOPY OF PUBLISHED WORK[21] *Cite published source fully, according to type, then add:* micro [film/fiche] no. [000], frame [000], Family History Library [FHL], Salt Lake City, Utah.[22]	**FHL MICROCOPY OF PUBLISHED WORK** *Cite unpublished source in short form recommended for that type of source, then add:* FHL. micro [film/fiche] [000,000], frame [000].	**FHL MICROCOPY OF PUBLISHED WORK** *Cite published source fully, according to type. Then add:* Micro [film/fiche]. Family History Library, Salt Lake City, Utah.
FHL MICROCOPY OF UNPUBLISHED MATERIAL[23] *Cite unpublished source fully, according to type, then add:* micro [film/fiche] no. [000,000], frame [000], Family History Library [FHL], Salt Lake City, Utah.	**FHL MICROCOPY OF UNPUBLISHED MATERIAL** *Cite unpublished source in short form recommended for that type of source, then add:* FHL. micro [film/fiche] [000,000], frame [000].	**FHL MICROCOPY OF UNPUBLISHED MATERIAL** *Cite unpublished source fully, according to type. Then add:* Micro [film/fiche]. Family History Library, Salt Lake City, Utah.

20. *Ancestral File*™ and *International Genealogical Index*™ are registered trademarks for databases created by the Family History Library. Regarding trademarks, once a product is thus identified in a publication, subsequent citations can dispense with the formality.

21. Examples include published books that have been filmed for distribution and National Archives microfilm publications.

22. Beginning in 1997, newly produced film at FHL will have frame numbers to facilitate citations.

23. Examples include county-level deeds, state-level tax rolls, federal tract books, church registers, and compiled manuscripts.

Primary Citation (Endnotes or Footnotes)	*Subsequent Citations* (Endnotes or Footnotes)	*Bibliographic Entry*
GOVERNMENT DOCUMENT *See also* LAW, NATIONAL ARCHIVES, *and specific types of documents created by local, state, and federal governments.*		
GOVERNMENT DOCUMENT (PUBLISHED) 1. Testimony of Marie S. Brevell, 16 September 1805, *The Debates and Proceedings of the Congress of the United States, Ninth Congress, First Session* (Washington: Gales and Seaton, 1852), 1211. This series, which has borne various titles over the centuries, is generically known as *Annals of Congress.*	**GOVERNMENT DOCUMENT (PUBLISHED)** 1. *Annals of Congress*, 9th Congress, 1st session, 1211.	**GOVERNMENT DOCUMENT (PUBLISHED)** United States Congress. *The Debates and Proceedings of the Congress of the United States, Ninth Congress, First Session.* Washington: Gales and Seaton, 1852.
INTERNATIONAL GENEALOGICAL INDEX™[24] [IGI] ENTRY 1. Orian Chase Shown entry, *International Genealogical Index [IGI]* (Salt Lake City: Family History Library, 1994), citing microfilm 1,396,190 for batch 8611901, sheet 95.		

24. An IGI entry is not an acceptable source in and of itself. It is only an *index entry*, not an actual record. Citations to an IGI entry should be considered highly temporary, at best—acceptable in research notes (but not published works) only until the original can be consulted. FHL cataloging commonly uses commas amid microfilm numbers but not in batch or fiche numbers.

Primary Citation (Endnotes or Footnotes)	Subsequent Citations (Endnotes or Footnotes)	Bibliographic Entry
INTERVIEW 1. Interview with Bessie (Shown) Dean (Mrs. James Dean; 79 Washington Street; Clarendon, AR 72029), by Elizabeth Shown Mills, 20 October 1968. Transcript held in 1996 by Mills (1732 Ridgedale Drive; Tuscaloosa, AL 35406). Mrs. Dean is now deceased.	**INTERVIEW** 1. Interview, Bessie (Shown) Dean, 20 October 1968.	**INTERVIEW** Dean, Bessie (Shown), interview. 20 October 1968, at 79 Washington Street; Clarendon, AR 72029. Transcript held in 1996 by interviewer, Elizabeth Shown Mills; 1732 Ridgedale Drive; Tuscaloosa, AL 35406-1942.
LAW, FEDERAL 1. "An Act to regulate trade and intercourse with the Indian tribes," 30 March 1802, chapter 14, 7th Congress, 1st session, in Richard Peters, editor, *The Public Statutes at Large of the United States of America*, 8 volumes (Boston: Charles C. Little and James Brown, 1845), 2: 139–46.	**LAW, FEDERAL** 1. "Act to regulate trade with the Indian tribes," 30 March 1802, 7th Congress, 1st session.	**LAW, FEDERAL** Peters, Richard, editor. *The Public Statutes at Large of the United States of America*, 8 volumes. Boston: Charles C. Little and James Brown, 1845.
LAW, STATE 1. "An Act for the Maintenance and support of illegitimate children," 2 February 1824, Joseph R. Swan, compiler, *Revised Statutes, State of Ohio, in Force, 1 Aug. 1860* (Cincinnati: Robert Clarke and Company, 1869), chapter 15.	**LAW, STATE** 1. "Act for . . . illegitimate children," 2 February 1824, in Swan, *Revised Statutes, State of Ohio . . . 1860*, chapter 15.	**LAW, STATE** Swan, Joseph R., compiler. *Revised Statutes, State of Ohio, in Force, 1 Aug. 1860*. Cincinnati: Robert Clarke and Company, 1869.

Primary Citation (Endnotes or Footnotes)	Subsequent Citations (Endnotes or Footnotes)	Bibliographic Entry
LECTURE (TAPED) 1. Donna Rachal Mills, "Finding 'Lost' American Ancestors in British and Spanish Florida" (lecture, annual conference, National Genealogical Society [NGS], Houston, Texas, May 1994); audiocassette recording available as Houston S-195 (Hobart, Indiana: Repeat Performance, 1994). **LEGAL CASE (PUBLISHED REPORT) [25]** 1. François X. Martin, *Term Reports of Cases Argued and Determined in the Superior Court of the Territory of Orleans, 1809–1823*, 12 volumes (New Orleans: F. X. Martin, 1854), 1: 183; hereinafter, *Adelle v. Beauregard*, 1 Martin La. 183 (1810).[26]	**LECTURE (TAPED)** 1. Mills, "Finding 'Lost' American Ancestors in British and Spanish Florida," NGS lecture, 1994. **LEGAL CASE (PUBLISHED REPORT)** 1. *Adelle v. Beauregard*, 1 Martin La. 183 (1810).[26]	**LECTURE (TAPED)** Mills, Donna Rachal. "Finding 'Lost' American Ancestors in British and Spanish Florida." Lecture, annual conference, National Genealogical Society, Houston, Texas, May 1994. Audiocassette tape, Houston S-195. Hobart, Indiana: Repeat Performance, 1994. **LEGAL CASE (PUBLISHED REPORT)** Martin, François X. *Term Reports of Cases Argued and Determined in the Superior Court of the Territory of Orleans, 1809–1823*. 12 volumes. New Orleans: F. X. Martin, 1854.

25. Style manuals show considerable variations in the citation of published legal cases. As a rule, *The Chicago Manual of Style* uses a simpler format than *Harvard Blue Book*. The "subsequent citation" above follows *CMS*, and many publications use no citation other than this short form. However, researchers without legal training commonly need the full citation, shown in columns 1 and 3, in order to locate a specific volume. States are abbreviated in legal citations, as a rule.

26. Compare the manner of abbreviation used for the state in this shortened citation to the state "abbreviation" used in the interview format on the prior page. The interview mentions the state amid an address, and the U.S. Postal Service prefers the use of its *two-letter postal code* when writing addresses. However, most style manuals still dictate the use of the *standard state abbreviations* in general writing.

Primary Citation (Endnotes or Footnotes)	Subsequent Citations (Endnotes or Footnotes)	Bibliographic Entry
LEGAL CASE (UNPUBLISHED) 1. *Samuel Hook v. Thomas James*, Superior Court Records, 1822–33, Book (Box) 3: 97, Arkansas History Commission, Little Rock.	**LEGAL CASE (UNPUBLISHED)** 1. *Hook v. James*, Superior Court Book (Box) 3: 97, Arkansas History Commission.	**LEGAL CASE (UNPUBLISHED)** Arkansas. Arkansas History Commission, Little Rock. Superior Court Records, 1822–33.
LETTER (ANNOTATED CITATION) 1. Letter from Maude (King) Hawkins (Mrs. R. O. Hawkins; Route 2; Cedar Vale, KS 67024) to Elizabeth Shown Mills, 16 April 1972; held in 1996 by Mills (1732 Ridgedale Drive; Tuscaloosa, AL 35406). The late Mrs. Hawkins was granddaughter to the couple she discusses.	**LETTER (ANNCTATED CITATION)** 1. Letter, Maude (King) Hawkins to Elizabeth Shown Mills, 16 April 1972.	**LETTER (ANNOTATED CITATION)** Hawkins, Maude (King), letter. 16 April 1972, from Route 2; Cedar Vale, KS 67024, to Elizabeth Shown Mills. Held in 1996 by Mills; 1732 Ridgedale Drive; Tuscaloosa, AL. 35406–1942.
LINEAGE APPLICATION 1. Lineage application of Priscilla Anne Scabery Anderson, national no. 651950, National Society, Daughters of the American Revolution, supplemental (Captain Thomas Anderson), "Add" volume 674, approved 1988.[27]	**LINEAGE APPLICATION** 1. DAR supplemental, Priscilla Anne Scabery Anderson, national no. 651950, "Add" volume 674.	**LINEAGE APPLICATION** Daughters of the American Revolution, National Society, Washington, D.C. Supplemental application of Priscilla Anne Scabery Anderson, national no. 651950, "Add" volume 674.

27. Various lineage societies have their own preferred styles for citing their materials. A safe policy is to ask for a style guide from the particular organization whose records you are using.

Primary Citation (Endnotes or Footnotes)	Subsequent Citations (Endnotes or Footnotes)	Bibliographic Entry
MANUSCRIPT (FILMED FOR DISTRIBUTION) 1. *Southern Women and Their Families in the 19th Century: Papers and Diaries; Part 6, Virginia;* micropublication, 30 rolls (Bethesda, Maryland: University Publications of America, 1992), roll 1, frame 123, document 2.	**MANUSCRIPT (FILMED FOR DISTRIBUTION)** 1. *Southern Women . . . 19th Century: Papers and Diaries . . . Virginia;* roll 1, frame 123, document 2.	**MANUSCRIPT (FILMED FOR DISTRIBUTION)** *Southern Women and Their Families in the 19th Century: Papers and Diaries; Part 6, Virginia.* Micropublication. Bethesda, Maryland: University Publications of America, 1992. Roll 1.
MANUSCRIPT (FILMED, LIMITED DISTRIBUTION) 1. Jackson County, Tennessee, Ranger Book, 1817–60: 21; microfilm 024,706, Family History Library [FHL], Salt Lake City, Utah.	**MANUSCRIPT (FILMED, LIMITED DISTRIBUTION)** 1. Jackson County, Tennessee, Ranger Book, 1817–60: 21; FHL microfilm 024,706.	**MANUSCRIPT (FILMED, LIMITED DISTRIBUTION)** Jackson County, Tennessee. Ranger Book, 1817–60. Microfilm 024,706. Family History Library, Salt Lake City, Utah.
MANUSCRIPT (UNFILMED) 1. John Ball to Thomas Massie, letter, 14 April 1792, MS M385525, Massie Papers, Virginia Historical Society, Richmond.	**MANUSCRIPT (UNFILMED)** 1. John Ball to Thomas Massie, letter, 14 April 1792, Massie Papers.	**MANUSCRIPT (UNFILMED)** Ball, John, to Thomas Massie. Letter, 14 April 1792. MS M385525, Massie Papers, Virginia Historical Society, Richmond.
MAP (HISTORIC) 1. Henry Popple, *A Map of the British Empire in America; with the French, Spanish and Hollandish Settlements Adjacent Thereto* (Amsterdam: I. Covens and C. Mortier, 1733), color map, 49 x 48 cm. Copy at Birmingham, Alabama, Public Library.	**MAP (HISTORIC)** 1. Popple, *Map of the British Empire in America; with the . . . Settlements Adjacent,* 1733.	**MAP (HISTORIC)** Popple, Henry. *A Map of the British Empire in America; with the French, Spanish and Hollandish Settlements Adjacent Thereto.* Amsterdam: I. Covens and C. Mortier, 1733.

Primary Citation (Endnotes or Footnotes)	Subsequent Citations (Endnotes or Footnotes)	Bibliographic Entry
MAP (TOPOGRAPHIC) 1. U.S. Department of the Interior, *Geological Survey Topographical Map; Virginia 1° block 38078; Luray Quadrangle, 7.5' Series* (Topographic), 38078–F4–TF–024: 91965, photo-revised 1987.	**MAP (TOPOGRAPHIC)** 1. *Geological Survey Topographical Map; Virginia . . . Luray Quadrangle, 7.5' series*, 1987.	**MAP (TOPOGRAPHIC)** United States. Department of the Interior, *Geological Survey Topographical Map; Virginia 1° block 38078; Luray Quadrangle, 7.5' Series* (Topographic). 1987.
MARRIAGE RECORD (CHURCH) *(Original record)* 1. Rogers-Morgan marriage, 2 November 1848, in Registre des Mariages 1 (original volume), unpaginated, arranged by date, St. John the Baptist Catholic Church, Cloutierville (Natchitoches Parish), Louisiana.	**MARRIAGE RECORD (CHURCH)** *(Original record)* 1. Registre des Mariages 1: entry for Rogers-Morgan, 2 November 1848, St. John the Baptist Church, Cloutierville.	**MARRIAGE RECORD (CHURCH)** *(Original record)* Louisiana. Natchitoches Parish. St. John the Baptist Catholic Church, Cloutierville. Marriage Registers.
(Certificate) 1. Rogers-Morgan marriage, 2 November 1848, St. John the Baptist Catholic Church, Cloutierville (Natchitoches Parish), Louisiana. Certificate supplied 1 June 1971 by Rev. M. J. Broussard, citing no book or page number; held in 1996 by Elizabeth Shown Mills (1732 Ridgedale Drive; Tuscaloosa, AL 35406).	*(Certificate)* 1. Certificate, Rogers-Morgan marriage of 2 November 1848.	*(Certificate)* Rogers-Morgan. Certificate of 1848 marriage. Natchitoches Parish, Louisiana. Issued 1971 by St. John the Baptist Catholic Church, Cloutierville. Copy held in 1996 by Elizabeth Shown Mills; 1732 Ridgedale Drive; Tuscaloosa, AL 35406-1942.

Primary Citation (Endnotes or Footnotes)	Subsequent Citations (Endnotes or Footnotes)	Bibliographic Entry
MARRIAGE RECORD (CHURCH), CONT. *(Copy, copyist known)* 1. Henry James Young, translator, "Register of York Springs Lutheran Church, Adams County, Pennsylvania" (typescript, 1939; in York Historical Society, York), 95.	**MARRIAGE RECORD (CHURCH), CONT.** *(Copy, copyist known)* 1. Young, "Register of York Springs Lutheran Church," 95.	**MARRIAGE RECORD (CHURCH), CONT.** *(Copy, copyist known)* Young, Henry James, translator. "Register of York Springs Lutheran Church, Adams County, Pennsylvania." 1939 typescript. York Historical Society, York.
(Copy, copyist unknown) 1. Rogers-Morgan marriage, 2 November 1848, in Marriage Book 1 (Latin copy): entry 72, Saint John the Baptist Catholic Church, Cloutierville (Natchitoches Parish), Louisiana.	*(Copy, copyist unknown)* 1. Marriage Book 1 (Latin copy): entry 72, Saint John the Baptist Catholic Church.	*(Copy, copyist unknown)* Louisiana. Natchitoches Parish. Saint John the Baptist Catholic Church, Cloutierville. Marriage Registers.
MARRIAGE RECORD (CIVIL) 1. Laramie County Marriage Book 3: 2, County Clerk's Office, Cheyenne, Wyoming.	**MARRIAGE RECORD (CIVIL)** 1. Laramie County Marriage Book 3: 2.	**MARRIAGE RECORD (CIVIL)** Wyoming. Laramie County. County Clerk's Office, Cheyenne. Marriage Registers.
MILITARY RECORD (MANUSCRIPT) 1. "Muster Roll of a Recruiting Party and Recruits Commanded by Brevet Major J. Selden, 8th Infantry, 29 February 1856–30 April 1856," box 220, Inspection Returns, 1821–60, Recruiting, New York; Office of the Adjutant General, Record Group 94; National Archives, Washington.	**MILITARY RECORD (MANUSCRIPT)** 1. "Muster Roll . . . 8th Infantry, 29 February 1856–30 April 1856."	**MILITARY RECORD (MANUSCRIPT)** United States. National Archives, Washington. Office of the Adjutant General. Record Group 94. Inspection Returns, 1821–60, box 220. Recruiting.

Primary Citation (Endnotes or Footnotes)	Subsequent Citations (Endnotes or Footnotes)	Bibliographic Entry
MILITARY-SERVICE FILE (FILMED) 1. James P. Drew, compiled military record (private, Company C, Purnell's Legion, Cavalry), *Compiled Service Records of Volunteer Union Soldiers Who Served in Organizations from the State of Maryland*, micropublication M384 (Washington: National Archives), roll 40. **[NA] NATIONAL ARCHIVES[28]** *See also* BOUNTY-LAND FILE, CENSUS, MILITARY RECORD, NATURALIZATION RECORD, *and* PENSION FILE. **NA FILM/FICHE (BASIC FORM)** 1. [*Specific document name*]; [*file name/number or page/line number, if relevant*]; [*microfilm title, if relevant*]; [*microfilm title, in italics; publication number*] (Washington: National Archives), [*roll or fiche number*], [*frame number*].	**MILITARY-SERVICE FILE (FILMED)** 1. James P. Drew, *Compiled Service Records . . . Union Soldiers . . . Maryland*, roll 40. **NA FILM/FICHE (BASIC FORM)** 1. [*Specific document name*]; [*microfilm title*], [*roll number*], [*frame number*].	**MILITARY-SERVICE FILE (FILMED)** *Compiled Service Records of Volunteer Union Soldiers Who Served in Organizations from the State of Maryland.* Micropublication M384, roll 40. Washington: National Archives. **NA FILM/FICHE (BASIC FORM)** [*Microfilm name, publication number*]. Washington: National Archives. [*Roll or fiche number.*]

28. Other formats for citing National Archives material appear in each issue of *Prologue: Journal of the National Archives* and in *Citing Records in the National Archives of the United States*, General Information Leaflet no. 17 (Washington: Government Printing Office [latest revision]). *Prologue* commonly uses a simpler form than the pamphlet recommends. Also note that National Archives microfilm may not carry a publication date in NA catalogs and other sources, although a filming date appears on each roll.

Primary Citation (Endnotes or Footnotes)	Subsequent Citations (Endnotes or Footnotes)	Bibliographic Entry
NA MANUSCRIPT (BASIC FORM) 1. [*Specific document name*], [*file/page number*], [*file name/number*], [*series title*]; [*record-group title/number*], National Archives, Washington.	**NA MANUSCRIPT (BASIC FORM)** 1. [*Specific document name*], [*file/page number*]; [*file name/number*], [*series title*], [*record-group title*], National Archives.	**NA MANUSCRIPT (BASIC FORM)** United States. National Archives, Washington. [*Record-group title/number*]. [*Series title*], [*file name/number*]. [*Specific document name/number*].
NA REGIONAL (UNOFFICIAL FILM HOLDINGS)²⁹ 1. Labon Gromer household, 1865 Kansas state census, population schedule, Johnson County, Shawnee township, Shawnee post office, page 131, dwelling 839, family 909; National Archives–Kansas City, microcopy Xc5, roll 4.	**NA REGIONAL (UNOFFICIAL FILM HOLDINGS)** 1. 1865 Kansas state census, population schedule, Johnson County, Shawnee township, page 131, dwelling 839, family 909. [*Or abbreviate appropriately.*]	**NA REGIONAL (UNOFFICIAL FILM HOLDINGS)** Kansas. Johnson County. State Census, 1865. Population schedule. National Archives–Kansas City microcopy Xc5, roll 4.
NATURALIZATION RECORD 1. Salvatore Ebettino, declaration of intention, case 8062 (1914); and petition for naturalization, case 5009 (1916); Supreme Court of New York, County of Westchester; Westchester County Records Center and Archives, Elmsford, New York.	**NATURALIZATION RECORD** 1. Supreme Court naturalizations, cases 8062 (1914) and 5009 (1916), Westchester County, New York.	**NATURALIZATION RECORD** New York. Westchester County. Westchester County Records Center and Archives, Elmsford. Supreme Court Naturalizations, cases 8062 (1914) and 5009 (1916).

29. Most National Archives micropublications are distinguishable by numbers beginning with *M* and *T*. A number of differently designated (not officially published) film holdings exist on site in the DC area facilities and the thirteen regional archives which treat specialized materials, confidential files, and (as in the Kansas example) gifts from other agencies and individuals.

Primary Citation (Endnotes or Footnotes)	*Subsequent Citations* (Endnotes or Footnotes)	*Bibliographic Entry*
NEWSPAPER CLIPPING (UNIDENTIFIED) (WITH PROVENANCE AND ANALYSIS) 1. "Pelagie Boyer. The Death of a Venerable Lady Born in St. Louis at the Beginning of the Present Century," undated clipping from unidentified newspaper, in family papers of Henriette (Bertrand) Charleville (Mrs. Joseph Charleville) of Cloutierville, Louisiana; inherited 1940 by her daughter Minerva (Charleville) Mills (Mrs. Hugh Mills) of Woodlawn, Texas; owned 1996 by Mrs. Mills's grandson, Gary B. Mills (1732 Ridgedale Drive; Tuscaloosa, AL 35406). This source is hereinafter cited as: Pelagie Boyer obituary. The style of the writing, the description of Mme. Boyer as "Venerable" and the reference to her birth "at the Beginning of the Present Century," all imply that the obituary was published in the latter part of the 1800s.	**NEWSPAPER CLIPPING (UNIDENTIFIED) (WITH PROVENANCE AND ANALYSIS)** 1. Pelagie Boyer obituary, previously discussed.	**NEWSPAPER CLIPPING (UNIDENTIFIED) (WITH PROVENANCE AND ANALYSIS)** Boyer, Pelagie. "The Death of a Venerable Lady Born in St. Louis at the Beginning of the Present Century." Undated clipping, c. late 1800s, from unidentified newspaper. Owned 1996 by Gary B. Mills; 1732 Ridgedale Drive; Tuscaloosa, AL 35406.
OBITUARY/NEWSPAPER ITEM 1. Andrzej Gutowski obituary, *Dziennik Polski* (Polish Daily News), Detroit, Michigan, 1 February 1939, page 7, column 1.	**OBITUARY/NEWSPAPER ITEM** 1. *Dziennik Polski*, 1 February 1939.	**OBITUARY/NEWSPAPER ITEM** *Dziennik Polski*. Detroit, Michigan, 1 February 1939.

Primary Citation (Endnotes or Footnotes)	Subsequent Citations (Endnotes or Footnotes)	Bibliographic Entry
PENSION FILE (FILMED) 1. Charles H. Ringgold file, no. WO 7830, *Case Files of Disapproved Pension Applications, 1861–1910;* micropublication M1274 (Washington: National Archives), fiche 002026.	**PENSION FILE (FILMED)** 1. Charles H. Ringgold, disapproved pension file, no. WO 7830, NARA M1274, fiche 002026.	**PENSION FILE (FILMED)** *Case Files of Disapproved Pension Applications, 1861–1910.* Micropublication M1274. Washington: National Archives.
PERIODICAL (ISSUED IN MULTIPLE SERIES) 1. [Anonymous], "Clopton Family," *William and Mary Quarterly,* series 1, volume 10 (July 1901): 54.	**PERIODICAL (ISSUED IN MULTIPLE SERIES)** 1. "Clopton Family," 54.	**PERIODICAL (ISSUED IN MULTIPLE SERIES)** "Clopton Family." *William and Mary Quarterly,* series 1, volume 10 (July 1901).
PHOTO, PORTRAIT, OR ILLUSTRATION (ARCHIVAL) (WITH ANNOTATION) 1. Nicolas Augustin Metoyer (1768–1856) portrait; life-size oil, signed "Feuille"; Saint Augustine Historical Society, Isle Brevelle (Natchitoches Parish), Louisiana. The portrait is undated and the artist unidentified, but the age and known life pattern of the subject (a wealthy freed slave and plantation owner) suggest that the portrait was painted about 1850.	**PHOTO, PORTRAIT, OR ILLUSTRATION (ARCHIVAL) (WITH ANNOTATION)** 1. Nicolas Augustin Metoyer portrait, Saint Augustine Historical Society.	**PHOTO, PORTRAIT, OR ILLUSTRATION (ARCHIVAL) (WITH ANNOTATION)** Metoyer, Nicholas Augustin. Portrait, c. 1850, Isle Brevelle, Louisiana. Saint Augustine Historical Society, Natchitoches Parish, Louisiana.
PHOTO, PORTRAIT, OR ILLUSTRATION (DIGITAL) *See* ELECTRONIC FILE.		

Primary Citation (Endnotes or Footnotes)	Subsequent Citations (Endnotes or Footnotes)	Bibliographic Entry
PHOTOGRAPH (PRIVATE POSSESSION) (ANNOTATED, WITH PROVENANCE) 1. Kate Chopin portrait, original, inscribed and signed on verso, "To Gabe — Taken Oct 25th 1870, Katie Chopin," with photographer's imprint on verso, "Scholten, Nos. 920 & 922 Olive Street, Cor. 10th Street, St. Louis, Mo." Photograph is 4¼" x 6½", card stock, brown tone. Gift by Kate to Gabrielle (Jamison) Charleville, Fiddletown, California (wife of Kate's great-uncle, F. A. Charleville). Inherited by Gabrielle's great-grandson, Charles King, Oakland, California. Gift by King in 1971 to Dr. and Mrs. Gary B. Mills. Owned 1996 by the Millses (1732 Ridgedale Drive; Tuscaloosa, AL 35406).	**PHOTOGRAPH (PRIVATE POSSESSION) (ANNOTATED, WITH PROVENANCE)** 1. Kate Chopin portrait, 1870, in possession of author.	**PHOTOGRAPH (PRIVATE POSSESSION) (ANNOTATED, WITH PROVENANCE)** Chopin, Kate. Portrait. 1870, St. Louis, Missouri. Owned 1996 by Dr. and Mrs. Gary B. Mills, 1732 Ridgedale Drive; Tuscaloosa, AL 35406.
PROBATE FILE 1. Anson B. Hathaway inventory, Ionia County probate file no. 1195 (Old Series), County Clerk's Office, Ionia, Michigan.	**PROBATE FILE** 1. Ionia County probate file no. 1195 (Old Series).	**PROBATE FILE** Michigan. Ionia County. County Clerk's Office, Ionia. Probate file 1195 (Old Series), 1862, Anson B. Hathaway.[30]

30. If only one file is used from a larger collection—as in the probate example above—the bibliographic entry should cite that specific file to make it clear that all files from the referenced period were not studied. If an entire year (or other period) of records is examined, then it is appropriate to cite the collection for that full year or period.

Primary Citation (Endnotes or Footnotes)	Subsequent Citations (Endnotes or Footnotes)	Bibliographic Entry
PROBATE FILE **(LOCAL, REMOVED TO OTHER FACILITY)**[31] 1. William Tapp estate, Clay County probate file CF-15-42, box 58 (Old Series), in Probate Division, Clay County Archives and Historical Library, Liberty, Missouri.	**PROBATE FILE** **(LOCAL, REMOVED TO OTHER FACILITY)** 1. William Tapp estate, file CF-15-42, box 58 (Old Series), Clay County Archives.	**PROBATE FILE** **(LOCAL, REMOVED TO OTHER FACILITY)** Missouri. Clay County. Clay County Archives and Historical Library, Liberty. Probate file CF-15-42, box 58 (Old Series), William Tapp estate.
RESEARCH REPORT 1. "William Ball of Giles County, Tennessee—Report No. 2," 17 March 1990, Gale Williams Bamman, CG (Post Office Box 7016; Nashville, TN 37207), to R. C. Ball (5307 Imogene; Houston, TX 77096), page 14; copy held by present writer [or cite repository].	**RESEARCH REPORT** 1. Bamman, "William Ball of Giles County, Tennessee—Report No. 2," 14.	**RESEARCH REPORT** Bamman, Gale Williams, CG. "William Ball of Giles County, Tennessee—Report No. 2," to R. C. Ball; 5307 Imogene; Houston, TX 77096. 17 March 1990. Copy held 1996 by present writer [or cite repository].
SERIES—BOOK (WITH SUBSETS) 1. *American State Papers: Documents Legislative and Executive of the Congress of the United States*, 38 volumes (Washington: Gales and Seaton, 1832–61), *Indian Affairs*, 2 volumes, 2: 25.	**SERIES—BOOK (WITH SUBSETS)** 1. *American State Papers, Indian Affairs*, 2: 25.	**SERIES—BOOK (WITH SUBSETS)** U.S. Congress. *American State Papers: Documents Legislative and Executive of the Congress of the United States*, 38 volumes. Washington: Gales and Seaton, 1832–61. *Indian Affairs*, 2 volumes.

31. Many local jurisdictions are transferring their materials to other archives that offer better preservation. In such cases, it is best to identify the record by the facility that holds the originals, as well as by the county/city of creation.

Primary Citation (Endnotes or Footnotes)	Subsequent Citations (Endnotes or Footnotes)	Bibliographic Entry
SHIP PASSENGER LIST (FILMED) 1. Gustov Kleine entry; SS *Imperator* Passenger Manifest, 17 September 1913, page 5, line 2; in *Passenger and Crew Lists of Vessels Arriving at New York, June 16, 1897–December 31, 1942*; micropublication T715 (Washington: National Archives), roll 2179.	**SHIP PASSENGER LIST (FILMED)** 1. Gustov Kleine, SS *Imperator* Passenger Manifest, 17 September 1913; NA T715, roll 2179.	**SHIP PASSENGER LIST (FILMED)** *Passenger and Crew Lists of Vessels Arriving at New York, June 16, 1897–December 31, 1942.* Micropublication T715, roll 2179. Washington: National Archives.
SOCIAL SECURITY DEATH INDEX [SSDI] 1. Paul Hoffman, no. 497–14–0553, Social Security Death Index, *FamilySearch* (Salt Lake City: Family History Library, 1994). The SSDI component of *FamilySearch* is drawn from the *Social Security Death Benefits Index* of the U.S. Social Security Administration.[32]	**SOCIAL SECURITY DEATH INDEX [SSDI]** 1. Paul Hoffman, no. 497–14–0553, Social Security Death Index, *FamilySearch*.	**SOCIAL SECURITY DEATH INDEX [SSDI]** Social Security Death Index, *FamilySearch*. Salt Lake City: Family History Library, 1994.
SYLLABUS MATERIAL 1. Michael P. Palmer, "German Church and Civil Records," *A Chesapeake Homecoming*, 1993 Conference Syllabus, National Genealogical Society (Arlington, Virginia: NGS, 1993), 344–47.	**SYLLABUS MATERIAL** 1. Palmer, "German Church and Civil Records," 344–47.	**SYLLABUS MATERIAL** Palmer, Michael P. "German Church and Civil Records," *A Chesapeake Homecoming*. 1993 Conference Syllabus, National Genealogical Society (Arlington, Virginia: NGS, 1993).

32. *FamilySearch*™ is a registered trademark of the Family History Library. If the SSDI is accessed through an electronic database other than *FamilySearch*, the citation of the other source should appear in lieu of the *FamilySearch* citation.

Primary Citation (Endnotes or Footnotes)	*Subsequent Citations* (Endnotes or Footnotes)	*Bibliographic Entry*
TAX ROLL (FILMED, LIMITED DISTRIBUTION) (CONSULTED OFF-SITE) 1. Samuel Clement entry, 1796 Tax Digest, Alexander's District, entry 53, Jefferson County, Georgia; microcopy RHS 953–54; Georgia Department of Archives and History, Atlanta.	**TAX ROLL (FILMED, LIMITED DISTRIBUTION) (CONSULTED OFF-SITE)** 1. Jefferson County, 1796 Tax Digest.	**TAX ROLL (FILMED, LIMITED DISTRIBUTION) (CONSULTED OFF-SITE)** Georgia. Jefferson County. Tax Digest, 1796. Georgia Department of Archives and History, Atlanta.
TAX ROLL (UNFILMED) 1. S. E. Harrison entry, Perry County 1861 Tax Roll, Old Town Beat, page 63; Probate Judge's Office (Basement Storage), Marion, Alabama.	**TAX ROLL (UNFILMED)** 1. Perry County 1861 Tax Roll, Old Town Beat, 63.	**TAX ROLL (UNFILMED)** Alabama. Perry County. Tax Rolls, 1861. Probate Judge's Office, Marion.
THESIS 1. Elizabeth Shown Mills, "Family and Social Patterns of the Colonial Louisiana Frontier: A Quantitative Analysis, 1714–1803" (Senior Thesis, University of Alabama–New College, 1981), 231.	**THESIS** 1. Mills, "Family and Social Patterns," 231.	**THESIS** Mills, Elizabeth Shown. "Family and Social Patterns of the Colonial Louisiana Frontier: A Quantitative Analysis, 1714–1803." Senior Thesis, University of Alabama–New College, 1981.
TOWN RECORD 1. Claremont Town Records, Book 1: 236, City Clerk's Office, Claremont, New Hampshire.	**TOWN RECORD** 1. Claremont Town Records, Book 1: 236.	**TOWN RECORD** New Hampshire. Claremont. Town Records. City Clerk's Office, Claremont.

Primary Citation (Endnotes or Footnotes)	*Subsequent Citations* (Endnotes or Footnotes)	*Bibliographic Entry*
TOWN RECORD *See also* VITAL RECORD, DEED, WILL, *etc.*		
TRANSLATED WORK 1. Marcel Giraud, *A History of French Louisiana*, volume 1, *The Reign of Louis XIV, 1698–1715*, Joseph C. Lambert, translator (Baton Rouge: Louisiana State University Press, 1974), 227.	**TRANSLATED WORK** 1. Giraud. *History of French Louisiana* (Lambert, translator), 1: 227.	**TRANSLATED WORK** Giraud, Marcel. *A History of French Louisiana*, volume 1. *The Reign of Louis XIV, 1698–1715*, Joseph C. Lambert, translator. Baton Rouge: Louisiana State University Press, 1974.
TYPESCRIPT *See* DAR GENEALOGICAL RECORDS COMMITTEE REPORT *and* MARRIAGE RECORD (CHURCH), COPY.		
U.S. SERIAL SET *See* GOVERNMENT DOCUMENT *and* SERIES—BOOK.		
VIDEO 1. Robert A. Burns, *Out of Your Tree! Crazy about Genealogy,* VHS video (Austin, Texas: Rondo Films, 1993), minute 3.	**VIDEO** 1. Burns, *Out of Your Tree! Crazy about Genealogy* video, minute 3.	**VIDEO** Burns, Robert A. *Out of Your Tree! Crazy about Genealogy.* VHS video. Austin, Texas: Rondo Films, 1993.
VITAL RECORD (FILMED) Windsor, Connecticut, Vital Records, Book 1: 55, microfilm 1,316,427, Family History Library, Salt Lake City, Utah.	**VITAL RECORD (FILMED)** Windsor Vital Records, 1: 55.	**VITAL RECORD (FILMED)** Connecticut. Windsor. Vital Records. Microfilm. Family History Library, Salt Lake City, Utah.

Primary Citation (Endnotes or Footnotes)	Subsequent Citations (Endnotes or Footnotes)	Bibliographic Entry
VITAL RECORD (PUBLISHED) 1. Caroline Lewis Kardell and Russell A. Lovell Jr., comps., *Vital Records of Sandwich, Massachusetts, to 1885*, 3 vols. (Boston: New England Historic Genealogical Society, 1996), 1: 84. Hereinafter cited as: *Sandwich VR* (published). **VITAL RECORD** *See also* BIBLE RECORD, BIRTH REGISTRATION, DEATH REGISTRATION, MARRIAGE RECORD. **WILL (RECORDED)** 1. John Dornblaser will (1805), Brooke County Will Book 1: 192, County Clerk's Office, Wellsburg, West Virginia. **WILL (UNRECORDED, CONSULTED OFF-SITE)** 1. Thomas Lea Sr. will (1844); Caswell County Loose Wills; file C.R.020.801.4, North Carolina Department of Archives and History, Raleigh.	**VITAL RECORD (PUBLISHED)** 1. *Sandwich VR* (published), 1: 84. **WILL (RECORDED)** 1. Brooke County Will Book 1: 192. **WILL (UNRECORDED, CONSULTED OFF-SITE)** 1. Thomas Lea Sr. will, Caswell County Loose Wills, North Carolina Archives.	**VITAL RECORD (PUBLISHED)** Kardell, Caroline Lewis and Russell A. Lovell Jr. *Vital Records of Sandwich, Massachusetts, to 1885.* 3 vols. Boston: New England Historic Genealogical Society, 1996. **WILL (RECORDED)** West Virginia. Brooke County. County Clerk's Office, Wellsburg. Will books, 1805. **WILL (UNRECORDED, CONSULTED OFF-SITE)** North Carolina. Caswell County. Loose Wills, 1844. Thomas Lea Sr. Department of Archives and History, Raleigh.

ppendixes

Sample: Documented Family Group Sheet

NO.	78 & 79	HUSBAND'S FULL NAME	Louis Solastie Rachal	

COMPILED BY (NAME & ADDRESS):		DATE	CITY/COUNTY	STATE/COUNTRY
Elizabeth Shown Mills, CG, CGL, FASG, FNGS	BIRTH	c. May 1797[1] c. 1792[2]	Cane River[1] Natchitoches Parish[2]	Louisiana[1,2]
1732 Ridgedale Drive	BAPTISM	18 Oct 1799[1]	Sponsors: Simeon & Marie Rachal[1]	
Tuscaloosa, AL 35406-1942	MARRIAGE	— — 1817[2]	Natchitoches Parish[2]	La.[2]
	DEATH	— Dec 1835[3]	Cane River[3]	La.[3]
	BURIAL	— Dec 1835[3]	Wise Cemetery, Marco, Natch. Parish[4]	La.[3]
	OCCUPATION	Planter (1835)[3]	RELIGION Roman Catholic[1,2] LITERACY Yes : French[2]	
	MILITARY	None known		
	OTHER WIVES	2: Marie Cephise Brosset[5] 30 Apr 1827 (civil)[5] 15 Feb 1829 (church)[5] Natch. Parish, La.[5]		
DATE: 1 January 1983	FATHER	Antoine Rachal[1,2,5]	MOTHER Marie Louise LeMoine[1,2,5]	

		WIFE'S FULL NAME	Marie Heloïse Botien dit St. André	
SPECIAL NOTES:	BIRTH	— May[6] 1802[2,6]	Monet's Bluff[6] Natchitoches Parish[6]	La.[1-2]
Marie Florentine and her mother both had tu-	BAPTISM	19 Nov 1804[6]	Sponsors: Jean Pierre Cloutier & Adrienne St. André[6]	
berculosis. Florentine's French-born husband	DEATH	late 1825 – 7 Jan 1826[7]	Cane River[7] Natchitoches Parish[3]	La.[7]
took her to France for medical treatment in the	BURIAL		Wise Cemetery, Marco,[4] Natch. Parish[4]	La.[3]
hospital that his family had founded.[18] See	OCCUPATION	Housewife	RELIGION Roman Catholic[2,6] LITERACY Status unknown	
Bertrand Papers for documents treating the	OTHER HUSBANDS			
family's history in medicine.[15]	FATHER	André[2,6] Botien[13] dit St. André[2,6]	MOTHER Marie Jacob Rachal[2,6]	

CHILDREN		DATE	CITY/COUNTY	STATE
	BIRTH	— May 1818[10]	Cane River[8] Natchitoches Parish[10]	La.[8]
1. Marie Melisa[10]	MARRIAGE	none		
SPOUSE:	DEATH	bef Jan 1836[7]	Cane River[8]	La.[6]
	BAPT./SPONS.	27 Jun 1818[10]	Manuel Rachal & Manette Rachal[10]	
	BIRTH	02 Dec 1819[10]	Cane River[8]	La.[8]
2. Marie Clarisa[10]	MARRIAGE	none		
SPOUSE:	DEATH	c. 1826–1828[7,9]	Cane River[8]	La.[6]
	BAPT./SPONS.	17 Mar 1820[10]	André St. André & Marie Louise Lemoine[10]	
	BIRTH	29 Nov 1821[10]	Cane River[10]	La.[10]
3. Marie Henriette[3,7,10,11]	MARRIAGE	30 Apr 1839[11]	Cloutierville[11] Natchitoches Parish[11]	La.[11]
SPOUSE: Joseph LaRoux[11]	DEATH	aft May 1864[12]		
	BAPT./SPONS.	22 May 1825[10,19]	Sylvestre Rachal & Marie Rose Zoriche[10,10]	
	BIRTH	06 Apr 1823[10]	Cane River[8]	La.[18]
4. Marie Florentine[13,7,10,14]	MARRIAGE	03 Mar 1842[14]	Cloutierville[14]	La.[14]
SPOUSE: Charles Claude Bertrand[14]	DEATH	31 May 1855[15]	Couches-les-Mines,[15] Saone-et-Loire[15]	France[15]
	BAPT./SPONS.	22 May 1825[10,19]	Sylvestre Rachal "paternal uncle," & Marie Rose Zoriche[10,19]	
	BIRTH	— — 1825[16,17]	Cane River[8]	La.[8]
5. Louis Honoré[16,17]	MARRIAGE	none		
SPOUSE:	DEATH	c.1826–1828[16,17]	Cane River[8]	La.[8]
	BAPT./SPONS.			

SOURCES:
1. Elizabeth Shown Mills, *Natchitoches, 1729–1803: [Translated] Abstracts of the Catholic Church Records* (New Orleans: Polyanthos, 1976), no. 2923.
2. Register 5, no. 1817: 10, St. François Church, Natchitoches [now Immaculate Conception].
3. Succession 429 (1835), Louis Solastie Rachal, Clerk of Court's Office, Natchitoches Parish Courthouse.
4. Located in section 59, township 7 N, range 5 W, Natchitoches Parish; read 1969 by Elizabeth Shown Mills.
5. Register 11, no. 2-1829, St. François.
6. Elizabeth Shown Mills, *Natchitoches, 1803–1826: Translated Abstracts . . . Parish of St. François . . .* (New Orleans: Polyanthos, 1980), no. 121.
7. Succession 72 (1826), Marie Heloise St. André (Mme. Solastie Rachal), Natchitoches Parish Courthouse.
8. Based upon parental residence at time of event.
9. Succession 128 (1828), André St. André, Natchitoches Parish Courthouse.
10. Register 19: Table of Baptisms, St. François. The original entry was made in Reg. 5, which is now heavily damaged. The entry is destroyed.
11. Register 8 [unnnumbered page, arranged by date], St. François. Reg. 8 is a baptismal book; a few marriages are randomly recorded there.
12. Testimony of Dr. S. O. Scruggs, *Bertrand v U.S.*, case no. 345, French & American Claims Commission, RG 79, National Archives, Washington.
13. Mills, *Natchitoches 1729–1803*, no. 2928.
14. Elizabeth Shown Mills, *Natchitoches Church Marriages: 1818–1850: Translated Abstracts . . .* (Tuscaloosa: Mills Historical Press, 1985), no. 527.
15. Death certificate of Marie Florentine Rachal (original copy), Charles Bertrand Papers, Louisiana State University Archives, Baton Rouge.
16. No priest was in the parish at the time of this birth.
17. Louis was named as youngest child in his mother's January 1826 succession. He was dead before the 1828 succession of his maternal grandfather.
18. Dora Minerva Charleville (Mrs. Hugh Eugene) Mills, Woodlawn, Texas, interview with, 1969. Mrs. Mills was granddaughter of Marie Florentine.
19. Reg. 19: Table of Baptisms, St. François, shows that Henriette and Florentine were baptized on same day, with same godparents. When Baptismal Book 1 was created for Cloutierville, from St. François records, Florentine's baptism was copied into the Cloutierville register; Henriette's was not.

APPENDIX 2
Sample: Documented Ancestor Chart

ANCESTOR CHART NO. ___4___

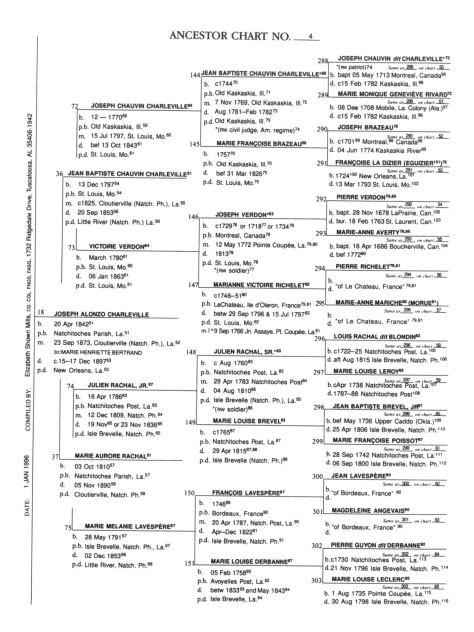

COMPILED BY:

DATE: 1 JAN 1996

18 JOSEPH ALONZO CHARLEVILLE
b. 20 Apr 1842[51]
p.b. Natchitoches Parish, La.[51]
m. 23 Sep 1873, Cloutierville (Natch. Ph.), La.[52]
to:MARIE HENRIETTE BERTRAND
d. c.15–17 Dec 1897[53]
p.d. New Orleans, La.[53]

72 JOSEPH CHAUVIN CHARLEVILLE[64]
b. 12 – 1770[59]
p.b. Old Kaskaskia, III.[59]
m. 15 Jul 1797, St. Louis, Mo.[60]
d. bef 13 Oct 1843[61]
p.d. St. Louis, Mo.[61]

36 JEAN BAPTISTE CHAUVIN CHARLEVILLE[61]
b. 13 Dec 1797[54]
p.b. St. Louis, Mo.[54]
m. c1825, Cloutierville (Natch. Ph.), La.[55]
d. 20 Sep 1853[56]
p.d. Little River (Natch. Ph.) La.[56]

73 VICTOIRE VERDON[64]
b. March 1780[61]
p.b. St. Louis, Mo.[60]
d. 06 Jan 1863[61]
p.d. St. Louis, Mo.[61]

74 JULIEN RACHAL, JR.[57]
b. 16 Apr 1786[63]
p.b. Natchitoches Post, La.[63]
m. 12 Dec 1809, Natch. Ph.[64]
d. 19 Nov[65] or 23 Nov 1836[65]
p.d. Isle Brevelle, Natch. Ph.[65]

37 MARIE AURORE RACHAL[51]
b. 03 Oct 1810[57]
p.b. Natchitoches Parish, La.[57]
d. 05 Nov 1890[58]
p.d. Cloutierville, Natch. Ph.[58]

75 MARIE MELANIE LAVESPÈRE[57]
b. 28 May 1791[67]
p.b. Isle Brevelle, Natch. Ph., La.[67]
d. 02 Dec 1853[68]
p.d. Little River, Natch. Ph.[69]

144 JEAN BAPTISTE CHAUVIN CHARLEVILLE*[59]
b. c1744[70]
p.b. Old Kaskaskia, III.[71]
m. 7 Nov 1769, Old Kaskaskia, III.[72]
d. Aug 1781–Feb 1782[73]
p.d. Old Kaskaskia, III.[73]
*(RW civil judge, Am. regime)[74]

145 MARIE FRANÇOISE BRAZEAU[59]
b. 1757[70]
p.b. Old Kaskaskia, III.[70]
d. bef 31 Mar 1826[75]
p.d. St. Louis, Mo.[75]

146 JOSEPH VERDON*[62]
b. c1729[76] or 1718[77] or 1734[78]
p.b. Montreal, Canada[79]
m. 12 May 1772 Pointe Coupée, La.[79,80]
d. 1813[78]
p.d. St. Louis, Mo.[78]
*(RW soldier)[77]

147 MARIANNE VICTOIRE RICHELET[62]
b. c1746–51[80]
p.b. LeChateau, Ile d'Oleron, France[79,81]
d. betw 29 Sep 1796 & 15 Jul 1797[82]
p.d. St. Louis, Mo.[82]
m.I*9 Sep 1766 Jn. Assaye, Pt. Coupée, La.[81]

148 JULIEN RACHAL, SR.*[63]
b. c Aug 1760[83]
p.b. Natchitoches Post, La.[83]
m. 29 Apr 1783 Natchitoches Post[84]
d. 04 Aug 1810[85]
p.d. Isle Brevelle (Natch. Ph.), La.[85]
*(RW soldier)[86]

149 MARIE LOUISE BREVEL[63]
b. c1765[87]
p.b. Natchitoches Post, La.[87]
d. 29 Apr 1815[87,88]
p.d. Isle Brevelle (Natch. Ph.)[88]

150 FRANÇOIS LAVESPÈRE[67]
b. 1746[89]
p.b. Bordeaux, France[90]
m. 20 Apr 1787, Natch. Post, La.[90]
d. Apr–Dec 1822[91]
p.d. Isle Brevelle, Natch. Ph.[91]

151 MARIE LOUISE DERBANNE[67]
b. 05 Feb 1758[92]
p.b. Avoyelles Post, La.[92]
d. betw 1833[93] and May 1843[94]
p.d. Isle Brevelle, La.[94]

288 JOSEPH CHAUVIN *dit* CHARLEVILLE*[72]
*(RW patriot)74   Same as 288 on chart 50
b. bapt 05 May 1713 Montreal, Canada[95]
d. c15 Feb 1782 Kaskaskia, III.[96]

289 MARIE MONIQUE GENEVIÈVE RIVARD[72]
b. 08 Dec 1708 Mobile, La. Colony (Ala.)[97]
d. c15 Feb 1782 Kaskaskia, III.[96]

290 JOSEPH BRAZEAU[75]
Same as 290 on chart 52
b. c1701[99] Montreal,[98] Canada[98]
d. 04 Jun 1774 Kaskaskia River[99]

291 FRANÇOISE LA DIZIER (EGUIZIER[101])[75]
Same as 291 on chart 53
b. 1724[100] New Orleans, La.[101]
d. 13 Mar 1793 St. Louis, Mo.[102]

292 PIERRE VERDON[79,80]
Same as 292 on chart 54
b. bapt. 28 Nov 1678 LaPrairie, Can.[102]
d. bur. 18 Feb 1763 St. Laurent, Can.[103]

293 MARIE-ANNE AVERTY[79,80]
Same as 293 on chart 55
b. bapt. 16 Apr 1686 Boucherville, Can.[104]
d. bef 1772[80]

294 PIERRE RICHELET[79,81]
Same as 294 on chart 56
b.
d. "of Le Chateau, France" [79,81]

295 MARIE-ANNE MARICHE[90] (MORUE[81])
Same as 295 on chart 57
b.
d. "of Le Chateau, France" [79,81]

296 LOUIS RACHAL *dit* BLONDIN[83]
Same as 296 on chart 58
b. c1722–25 Natchitoches Post, La.[105]
d. aft Aug 1815 Isle Brevelle, Natch. Ph.[106]

297 MARIE LOUISE LEROY[83]
Same as 297 on chart 59
b. cApr 1738 Natchitoches Post, La.[107]
d. 1787–88 Natchitoches Post[108]

298 JEAN BAPTISTE BREVEL, JR[87]
Same as 298 on chart 60
b. bef May 1736 Upper Caddo (Okla.)[109]
d. 25 Apr 1806 Isle Brevelle, Natch. Ph.[110]

299 MARIE FRANÇOISE POISSOT[87]
Same as 299 on chart 61
b. 28 Sep 1742 Natchitoches Post, La.[111]
d. 06 Sep 1800 Isle Brevelle, Natch. Ph.[112]

300 JEAN LAVESPÈRE[90]
Same as 300 on chart 62
b. "of Bordeaux, France" [90]
d.

301 MAGDELEINE ANGEVAIS[90]
Same as 301 on chart 63
b. "of Bordeaux, France" [90]
d.

302 PIERRE GUYON *dit* DERBANNE[92]
Same as 302 on chart 64
b. c1730 Natchitoches Post, La.[113]
d. 21 Nov 1796 Isle Brevelle, Natch. Ph.[114]

303 MARIE LOUISE LECLERC[92]
Same as 303 on chart 65
b. 1 Aug 1735 Pointe Coupée, La.[115]
d. 30 Aug 1798 Isle Brevelle, Natch. Ph.[116]

Sample: Documented Ancestor Chart
Reference Notes (cont.)

51. Book 9, Baptisms, 1840–1849, unpaginated, arranged by date; St. François Church (present Immaculate Conception), Natchitoches, La.

52. Marriages, 1855–1905 [original French], unpaginated, arranged by date; St. John the Baptist Church, Cloutierville, La.

53. Ecclesiastical Burials, A.D. 1847 to A.D. 1906 [original French], unpaginated, arranged by date; St. John the Baptist Church, Cloutierville.

54. Baptismal Certificate, Church of St. Louis (Old Cathedral), St. Louis, Missouri, provided 10 May 1972 by Rev. John J. Lang, with no citation of original book or page.

55. *Biographical and Historical Memoirs of Northwest Louisiana* (Nashville: Southern Publishing Co., 1890), 333, cites the year of marriage as 1825. Both church and civil marriage records of Natchitoches are missing for this year.

56. Grave marker, Cemetery of St. John the Baptist Church, Cloutierville.

57. Elizabeth Shown Mills, *Natchitoches, 1800–1826: Translated Abstracts of Register No. 5 of the Catholic Church Parish of St. François des Natchitoches in Louisiana* (New Orleans: Polyanthos, 1980), 62, no. 344, citing original p. 125.

58. "Ecclesiastical Burials, A.D. 1847 to A.D. 1906," unpaginated, arranged by date; St. John the Baptist Church, Cloutierville.

59. Registres, Notre-Dame de l'Immaculée Conception de Kaskaskias [Illinois], microcopy C-2224, Public Archives of Canada, Ottawa; see 1770 baptisms, arranged chronologically.

60. Marriage certificate, Church of St. Louis, prepared 10 May 1972 by Rev. John J. Lang; no citation of original book or page.

61. Obituary of Victoria Charleville, reprinted in biographical sketch of grandson Landry Charleville, *Biographical and Historical Memoirs of Northwest Louisiana*, 333–35.

62. 1860 U.S. cens., St. Louis Co., Mo. pop. sch., St. Louis, ward 3, p.161, dwell. 765, fam.1311; National Archives micropublication M432, roll 416.

63. Elizabeth Shown Mills, *Natchitoches, 1729–1803: Abstracts of the Catholic Church Registers of the French and Spanish Post of St. Jean Baptiste des Natchitoches in Louisiana* (New Orleans: Polyanthos, 1977), 224, no. 1905.

64. Mills, *Natchitoches, 1800–1826*, 160, no. 983.

65. Jacques Lacaze succession, Natchitoches Parish succ. file 139 (reporting death of Julien Rachal Jr., tutor of Lacaze minors), Clerk of Court's Office, Natchitoches.

66. Book 15, Deaths, 1793–96, 1827–49, unpaginated, arranged by date, St. François Church, Natchitoches.

67. Mills, *Natchitoches, 1729–1803*, 242, no. 2065.

68. "Cloutierville Yellow Fever List," *New Orleans Genesis* 35 (June 1970): 261–62; a reprint of a clipping from an unnamed newspaper. Local church registers are missing burial records between 1850 and 1857.

69. Place of death is based upon known residence at time of death.

70. No baptismal record has been found. Age is based upon the presumption that he was about 25 years and she was at least 15 years at time of marriage, these being typical ages for the place and time.

71. Birthplace is based upon known residence of parents during this decade. See Natalia Maree Belting, *Kaskaskia under the French Regime* (1948; reprinted, New Orleans: Polyanthos, 1975).

72. Registres, Notre-Dame de l'Immaculée Conception de Kaskaskias [Illinois]: 1769 marriages.

uidelines for
citing credentials* . . . .

Credentials are a worthy achievement for anyone engaged in the conduct or practice of genealogy. Properly used, they attest knowledge, skill, and ethics. They enhance credibility as a researcher, writer, consultant, lecturer, or court witness. They can facilitate access to records and repositories.

The Association of Professional Genealogists also recognizes that genealogical credentials are not widely known or understood in the public sector. Thus the public can be easily misled by an inappropriate use of postnomials implying special qualifications. To avoid misunderstandings and misinterpretations of the credentials held by genealogists, the association sets forth the following guidelines:

EDUCATIONAL CREDENTIALS

Earned credentials are appropriate descriptors of the researcher's educational background, within the following framework:

- If the degree is earned in a field other than genealogy, the genealogist should identify, in parentheses following the degree, the field in which the credential was earned.

- The degree should be granted by an accredited institution.

- Honorary degrees, as opposed to earned degrees, should not be presented as credentials.

PROFESSIONAL CREDENTIALS

Postnomials of a professional nature, earned outside the field of genealogy, may or may not be relevant, depending upon the circumstances:

- Postnomials earned in an adjunct field would be appropriate if the nature of one's genealogical work combines both fields (example: a genealogist with genetic-research credentials who lectures on the applicability of genealogy to genetics or seeks research assignments that focus on family-health issues).

---

*Adopted May 1995 by the Association of Professional Genealogists; Post Office Box 40393; Denver, CO 80204-0393. Used herein with permission.

- Outside this limited context, the genealogical use of nongenealogical credentials is commonly considered inappropriate.

Professional postnomials that imply genealogical expertise should be awarded by an accrediting or certifying body that

- conducts a rigorous examination program separate from membership in its own or another society; and

- publishes in professional genealogical literature and provides, in response to public requests, a clear and detailed explication of its examination policies and procedures—setting forth the specific standards that successful applicants must meet; and

- administers its tests on a non-exclusionary basis, without regard for race, creed, or color, and without need for personal recommendation by a current member of that agency; and

- makes public, upon request, its pass-fail ratio for applications in order to substantiate its high testing standards; and

- provides its applicants with an appraisal of the strengths and weaknesses of their applications, in support of its ruling for acceptance or rejection; and

- publishes, and makes available upon request, a roster of its approved genealogists; and

- does not usurp the preexisting credentials of any other testing agency.

HONORARY CREDENTIALS

Honorary postnomials, to have meaning, must denote exceptional expertise or service. As in other professional and scholarly fields, meaningful honorary postnomials are those

- awarded without application for the honor and without assessment of fees; and

- awarded by open-membership organizations to a very limited number of members, in recognition of noteworthy service (example: fellows of the National Genealogical Society, Utah Genealogical Association, or Genealogical Society of Pennsylvania); or

- awarded by scholastically oriented societies on the basis of published scholarship that has withstood peer review and public criticism—provided that such a society make public the specific criteria upon which its honorees are chosen and make available, upon request, its list of honorees.

Used within this framework, genealogical credentials will accurately reflect the high standards of expertise and ethics that underlie all legitimate professions.

CITATION GUIDES:

The Chicago Manual of Style. 14th edition. Chicago: University of Chicago Press, 1993.

Citing Records in the National Archives of the United States. General Information Leaflet no. 17. Washington: Government Printing Office [periodically revised].

Garner, Diane L. *The Complete Guide to Citing Government Information Resources: A Manual for Writers and Librarians*. Revised edition, Bethesda, Maryland: Congressional Information Service, 1993.

Gibaldi, Joseph. *MLA Handbook for Writers of Research Papers*. 4th edition, New York: Modern Language Association of America, 1995.

Hale, Constance. *Wired Style: Principles of English Usage in the Digital Age*. San Francisco: HardWired, 1996. Ongoing revision, online <www.hot wired.com/hardwired/wiredstyle/toc/index.html>.

Harnack, Andrew and Eugene Kleppinger. *Beyond the MLA Handbook: Documenting Electronic Sources on the Internet. Online* <english.ttu.edu/kairo/ 1.2/inbox/mla.html>. Eastern Kentucky University, Richmond, Kentucky.

Lackey, Richard S., CG, FASG. *Cite Your Sources: A Manual for Documenting Family Histories and Genealogical Records*. 1980; reprinted, Jackson: University Press of Mississippi, c1987.

Li, Xia and Nancy Crane. *Electronic Styles: A Handbook for Citing Electronic Information*. Medford, New Jersey: Information Today, 1996.

Library of Congress Catalog. Online <lcweb.loc.gov/catalog/>. Washington.

Mobley, Joe A. and Kathleen B. Wyche. *Guide for Authors and Editors*. Raleigh: Division of Archives and History, North Carolina Department of Cultural Resources, 1992.

Prologue: Quarterly of the National Archives. Published 1968 to date. (Its endnotes provide many useful models for concisely citing National Archives material.)

A Uniform System of Citation. 15th edition. Cambridge: Harvard Law Review Association, 1991. (Also known as *Harvard Blue Book.*)

University of Chicago Manual of Legal Citation. Rochester, New York: Lawyers Co-operative Publishing Company, 1989. (Also known as *The Maroon Book.*)

U.S. Government Printing Office. *A Manual of Style: A Guide to the Basics of Good Writing.* New York: Wings Books, 1986.

Walker, Janet and Todd Taylor. *The Columbia Guide to Online Style.* New York: Columbia University Press, 1998. Also partial guide at <www.cas.usf.edu/english/walker/mla.html>. University of South Florida, Tampa.

Whitley, Peggy. *MLA Style: Paper and Electronic* <www. nhmccd.edu/contracts/LRC/kc/mlastyle.html>. Kingswood College, Kingswood, Texas.

EVIDENCE-ANALYSIS GUIDES:

Evidence! A Special Issue of the National Genealogical Society Quarterly. Vol. 87, September 1999. (Introductory article by Elizabeth Shown Mills explores the latest principles of evidence analysis, as a supplement to *Evidence! Citation and Analysis for the Family Historian.* Four subsequent articles provide models for each of the four basic ways in which genealogists use complex evidence to resolve problems of identity and relationships.)

Federal Civil Judicial Procedure and Rules. 1995 edition. St. Paul, Minnesota: West Publishing Company, 1995.

Nickell, Joe, PH.D., CGRS. *Ambrose Bierce is Missing; And Other Historical Mysteries.* Lexington: University Press of Kentucky, 1991. (Demonstrates a variety of techniques to evaluate documents, resolve identities, and ferret out frauds.)

―――. *Camera Clues: A Handbook for Photographic Investigation.* Lexington: University Press of Kentucky, 1994.

―――. *Detecting Forgery: Forensic Investigation of Documents.* Lexington: University Press of Kentucky, 1996.

―――. *Pen, Ink, and Evidence: A Study of Writing and Writing Materials for the Penman, Collector, and Document Detective.* Lexington: University Press of Kentucky, 1991.

Stevenson, Noel C., J.D., FASG. *Genealogical Evidence: A Guide to the Standard of Proof Relating to Pedigrees, Ancestry, Heirship, and Family History.* Revised edition. Laguna Hills, California: Aegean Park Press, 1989.

RELATED GUIDES:

Board for Certification of Genealogists. *The BCG Standards Manual.* Salt Lake City: Ancestry.com, 2000.

"Copyright and Fair Use." Online <fairuse.stanford.edu>. Stanford University Libraries, Palo Alto, California.

Kozachek, Thomas. *Guidelines for Authors of Compiled Genealogies* [for the *New England Historical and Genealogical Register* and Newbury Street Press]. Boston: New England Historic Genealogical Society, 1998.

Curran, Joan Ferris; Madilyn Coen Crane; and John H. Wray. *Numbering Your Genealogy: Basic Systems, Complex Families, and International Kin.* National Genealogical Society Special Publication 64. Arlington, Virginia: NGS, 2000.

Hatcher, Patricia Law. *Producing a Quality Family History.* Salt Lake City: Ancestry, 1996.

———— and John V. Wylie. *Indexing Family Histories: Simple Steps for a Quality Product.* National Genealogical Society Special Publication 73. Arlington, Virginia: NGS, 1994.

Mills, Elizabeth Shown. "Skillbuilding: Analyzing and Reviewing Published Sources." *OnBoard: Newsletter of the Board for Certification of Genealogists* 3 (May 1997): 16.

————. "Skillbuilding: Producing Quality Research Notes." *OnBoard* 3 (January 1997): 8.

————. "Skillbuilding: Transcribing Source Materials." *OnBoard* 2 (January 1996): 8.

———— . "Your Research Report," *OnBoard* 2 (May 1996): 9–13.

———— and Gary B. Mills, with Robert C. Anderson, Jane Fletcher Fiske, David L. Greene, Henry B. Hoff, Sandra Hargreaves Luebking, and Harry Macy Jr., "Guidelines for Responsible Editing in Genealogy," *National Genealogical Society Quarterly* 84 (March 1996): 48–49.

ndex

ndex . . . .

Note:

The following index includes all names, references, and topics covered by the narrative discussions, figures, and explanatory notes. For the citation formats, it includes the topics but not the authors, sources, and repositories.

A

Derivative works
    analysis of 41, 44, 48–51, 55
Details, importance of 35
Devine, Donn 11
Diacritical marks, correcting 37
Diaries or journals
    analysis of 50, 52
    citation formats 26, 79, 88
    citation principles, 26
Direct evidence
    accumulation of 46
    analysis of 44–46
    definition of 45
Directories. *See* City (or County)
    directories
Discussional notes 18–20
Dissertations
    citation formats 79
    citation principles 40
Documentation guidelines 18
Duplicate records
    citation principles 31
    definition 49

E

E-mail
    citation formats 80
    citation principles 80
Editorial additions 40
Edited transcripts
    classification of 50
Electronic addresses
    citation principles 40, 80
Electronic data. *See also* Databases;
    Listserve messages; Web sites
    citation formats 72, 80
        quick chart 62
    citation principles 18, 32, 80
    special considerations 31
Electronic databases
    Ancestral File™ 64, 83
    FamilyFinder 72
    FamilySearch™ 97
    International Genealogical Index™
        83–84
    OCLC (On-line Computer Library
        Center) 35
    Social Security Death (Benefits)
        Index 97

Electronic images
    citation formats 80
Electronic publishing 35
    citation formats 82
Electronic re-recordings
    classification of 49
Ellipses 40, 66, 76
Endnotes 18
    definition of 24
    sequence of elements 63
Errors
    likelihood of 29, 43, 48–51
Ethical considerations 29–31, 106–
    7. *See also* Copyrights; Fair-use
    principle; Plagiarism
Evidence
    accumulation of direct 46
    assemblage of indirect 45–47, 57
    clear and convincing (legal) 47
    clearly convincing (genealogical)
        46–47
    conflicting 27–28, 43, 46–47
    derivative 49–51
    direct 44–46
    duplicates 49
    independently created 44, 48
    indirect 44–47, 57
    original 44, 48–49
    preponderance of 46–47
    primary 48
    secondary 48
Evidence analysis
    abstracts 50
    affidavits 52, 54–55
    baptismal records 55
    basic principles 42–58
    bible records 52, 54–55
    compendiums 50
    compilers, skills of 44, 50, 52–53
    correspondence 49
    custodial history of records
        44, 55–56
    damage claims 52
    death certificates 52
    deeds 51, 55
    degrees of processing 51
    derivative works 48–51
    diaries 50, 52
    duplicates 49

M

Macy, Harry 11
Mallory, Rudena Kramer 11
Manuscripts
    citation formats 83, 88
        quick chart 62
    citation principles 31, 40
    permission to publish 30
Maps
    citation formats 88
    citation principles 40
Marriage records
    analysis of 55
    citation formats 89–90, 105
McMillion, Lynn 11
Melchiori, Marie Varrelman 11
Memoirs 50. *See also* Diaries and
    journals
Microforms
    citation formats 79, 83, 105
    citation formats, quick chart 62
    citation principles 18, 31–35, 40
    problems with using 31–35, 56
Military records
    citation formats 90
Military service files
    citation formats 90
Mills, Gary B. 11
MLA Handbook 14
Motivation of record creators 44, 51
Multiple entities
    authors 41, 68
    places of publication 66
    sources for documentation 46, 48

N

Name gathering 20
National Archives
    citation practices of 34, 61, 91
    style manual 34
National Archives materials
    citation formats 71–72, 80, 82,
      90–91, 97
    citation principles 90–91
      manuscripts 34
      microforms 33–34
      regional facilities 92

National Union Catalog 35
Naturalization records
    citation formats 26, 92
Newspapers
    citation formats 93, 105
    citation practices of 40
    citation principles 39
Nolan, Joseph R. 47
Note numbers, placement of 25–27
Notes. *See* Discursive notes;
    Endnotes; Footnotes; Paren-
    thetical citations; Source notes
Numbering generations 26
Nurse, Howard 11

O

Obituaries
    analysis of 93
    citation formats 93, 105. *See also*
    Newspapers
OCLC (On-line Computer Library
    Center) 35
Online data. *See* Electronic data
Op. cit., use of 36
Oral information 49, 85
Original creator
    importance of identifying 32, 44,
     52–53
Original sources 29–30, 44, 48–51

P

Paper, analysis of 56
Parenthetical citations 18, 23–24
Passenger lists or rolls
    citation formats 97
    frauds 56
Penmanship
    analysis of 44, 54–55
    ancestral 54–55
    scribal 55
Pension applications
    analysis of 54
    citation formats 94
Periodicals. *See also* Articles
    citation formats 77, 94
Permissions for use
    manuscript materials 30
    published materials 30

U

U.S. postal codes 39, 86
U.S. Serial Set 99
U.S. *See also* National Archives,
    Bureau of . . . , *and various
    government record types*
Underscoring titles 63
Unknown authors 41, 67
Unpublished *v.* published materials
    citation principles 40, 63
    distinguishing between 37

V

Van der Rohe, Mies 35
Veracity of record creators 44, 50,
    52–53
Videos
    citation formats 99

Vital records
    citation formats 21, 100
    citation principles 21

W

Wallace, W. H. L. "Lew," General 53
Web sites. *See also* Appendix for
    Bibliography
    citation formats 80, 82
    Library of Congress 35
    National Archives 82
Weight of evidence 43–46
Whipp, Wendy 11
Wills
    analysis of 55
    citation formats 100
Written evaluations of evidence 47
Wylie, John V. 11